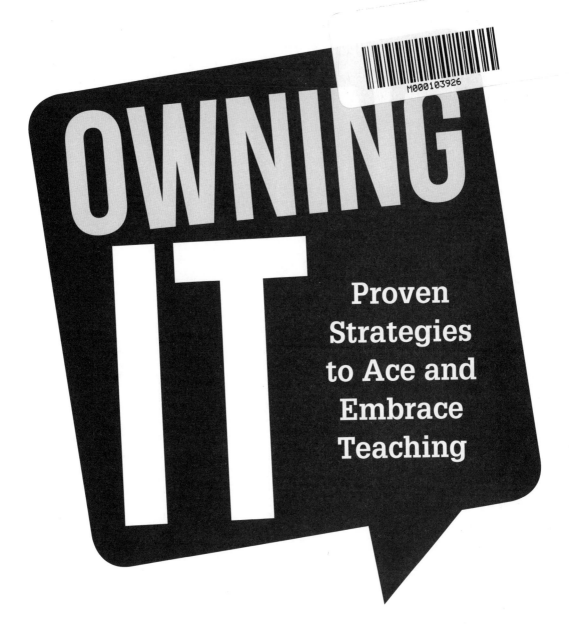

OWNING IT

Proven
Strategies
to Ace and
Embrace
Teaching

Alex Kajitani

Foreword by Harry K. Wong

Solution Tree | Press a division of
Solution Tree

555 North Morton Street
Bloomington, IN 47404
800.733.6786 (toll free) / 812.336.7700
FAX: 812.336.7790

email: info@SolutionTree.com
SolutionTree.com

Visit **go.SolutionTree.com/instruction** to download the free reproducibles in this book.

Printed in the United States of America

Library of Congress Cataloging-in-Publication Data

Names: Kajitani, Alex, author.
Title: Owning it : proven strategies to ace and embrace teaching / Alex
    Kajitani ; contributors, Mindy Crum, Pete Fisher, and Megan
    Pincus-Kajitani.
Description: Bloomington, IN : Solution Tree Press, [2018] | Includes
    bibliographical references and index.
Identifiers: LCCN 2018013705 | ISBN 9781947604117 (perfect bound)
Subjects: LCSH: Effective teaching--Methodology. | Academic achievement.
Classification: LCC LB1025.3 .K355 2018 | DDC 371.102--dc23 LC record available at
    https://lccn.loc.gov/2018013705

Solution Tree
Jeffrey C. Jones, CEO
Edmund M. Ackerman, President

Solution Tree Press
President and Publisher: Douglas M. Rife
Editorial Director: Sarah Payne-Mills
Art Director: Rian Anderson
Managing Production Editor: Kendra Slayton
Senior Production Editor: Todd Brakke
Senior Editor: Amy Rubenstein
Proofreader: Kendra Slayton
Text and Cover Designer: Abigail Bowen
Editorial Assistant: Sarah Ludwig

For my wonderful wife, Megan.

Here's to creating the world *as it can be*.

—Alex

ACKNOWLEDGMENTS

I am deeply grateful to the thousands of teachers, students, and parents I have come into contact with over my education career, a career which started the day I entered preschool. There is not a single person that I've met in that time who hasn't taught me something, and what I've learned is reflected in small and big ways in these pages. Also, to my wonderful wife, children, and family, I thank you from the depths of my soul. What is best in me, I owe to all of you.

Solution Tree Press would like to thank the following reviewers:

Tara Foster
Assistant Principal
Hueytown Middle School
Hueytown, Alabama

Katie McCann
Fifth-Grade Teacher
Appomattox Elementary School
Appomattox, Virginia

Clint Heitz
Instructional Coach
Bettendorf Community Schools
Bettendorf, Iowa

Jason Ince
Agriculture Teacher
Chatham High School
Chatham, Virginia

Kathy Hoover
CTE: Sports Medicine &
    Rehabilitation Services Teacher
Kofa High School
Yuma, Arizona

Heidi Trude
French Teacher
Skyline High School
Front Royal, Virginia

TABLE OF CONTENTS

Reproducible pages are in italics.

About the Author . . . .**xv**

   About the Contributors. xvi

Foreword by Harry K. Wong . . . .**xvii**

Introduction **1**

   What This Book Is 2

   How This Book Is Structured 3

      Part 1: Owning It in Your Classroom. 3

      Part 2: Owning It With Your Most Challenging Students 3

      Part 3: Owning It at Your School and District 4

      Part 4: Owning It in Your Community 5

   How to Use This Book. 5

PART 1

**Owning It in Your Classroom: Strategies for Creating an
Environment of Achievement** **7**

1 TIME TO GET REAL
Revisit Your Personal Philosophy's Value **9**

   What It Means to Be Real. 10

   Strategies for Success. 10

      Teach What Is Real 10

      Be Reliable. 11

      Be Realistic 11

   Summary. 12

   Reflection Questions *13*

2 FIRST IMPRESSIONS
Make the Most of the First Five Minutes of Any Class 15

    Students Are Your Customers 15

    Strategies for Success. 16

        Connect Quickly 16

        Lose the Lull 16

        Grab Their Attention 17

        Provide Purpose 18

        Cut the Hypocrisy. 18

    Summary. 19

    Reflection Questions *20*

3 VISIBILITY IS EVERYTHING
Increase Your Classroom Presence to Seem Like You're
Everywhere at Once 21

    The Broken-Windows Theory. 22

    Strategies for Success. 23

        Make Phone Calls Home 24

        Honk and Wave While Driving to School 24

        Greet Your Students at the Door 24

        Utilize the Eyes in the Back of Your Head. 25

        Insist on a Clean Floor 25

    Summary. 26

    Reflection Questions *27*

4 PLEASE STOP THINKING
Understand Four Things Teachers Say That Sabotage
Learning. 29

    Strategies for Success. 29

        Connect to What Students *Do* Know. 30

        Stress the Learning, Not the Testing 30

        Remember That the One Doing the Talking Is Often
           the One Doing the Learning 31

        Dig Deeper to Address the Issue Behind the Issue 33

    Summary. 34

    Reflection Questions *35*

5 I SAID BE QUIET . . . AND START TALKING
Help Students Learn Out Loud and Still Keep a Handle
on Your Classroom 37

    We Can't Fear Student Participation 38

    Strategies for Success. 39

Use Think-Pair-Share 39

Ask Three Questions 40

Record It 42

Summary 43

Reflection Questions *44*

6 DEAL WITH DATA
Transform Your Perception of Data and Help Your Students Succeed

. . . . 45

How We Define Data 46

Strategies for Success 47

Use Data to Begin a Conversation, Not to End It 47

See the Real Student Behind Every Piece of Data 48

Make Data Useful by Not Keeping Them Secret 49

Use Analogies to Make Data Friendly 49

Summary 51

Reflection Questions *52*

7 IT'S TEST TIME
Think Outside the Bubble on All-Important Standardized Tests

. . . . 53

Strategies for Success 54

Make It About Improvement, Not Perfection 54

Focus on Celebration, Not Intimidation 55

Involve the Whole School Community 56

Talk to Your Students About Bias in Testing 56

Summary 57

Reflection Questions *58*

PART 2

Owning It With Your Most Challenging Students: Strategies for Succeeding With Students Who Are Struggling or At Risk
. . . . 59

8 IT'S ABOUT TIME
Close the Achievement Gap With Struggling Students
. . . .61

Real Students in the Metaphorical Gap 62

Strategies for Success 63

Teach Curriculum That Is Culturally Relevant 63

Help Keep Other Good Teachers (Like You!) at Your School . . . 64

Get Targeted Training 64

Connect With the Quiet Ones 65

Summary 65

Reflection Questions 67

9 LET'S TALK ABOUT RACE
Bring Ethnic Identity and Culturally Relevant Curriculum Into Your Classroom 69

Where to Begin 70

Strategies for Success 71

Understand What Ethnicity Is 71

Understand How Ethnicity Forms 71

Understand How to Use Ethnicity in the Classroom 73

Summary 74

Reflection Questions 76

10 THE SECRET TO MOTIVATING THE UNMOTIVATED STUDENT
Succeed With Students Who Are At Risk 77

A Super Success Story 78

Strategies for Success 79

Understand and Honor Cultural Barriers 79

Bring in Success Stories 80

Tell Them About Yourself 80

Summary 81

Reflection Questions 82

11 BEYOND THE BAD KID with Pete Fisher
Manage Disruptive Classroom Behavior 83

What Lies Behind the Behavior 84

Strategies for Success 85

Maintain Your Self-Control 85

Create an Environment That Fosters Positive Behaviors 86

Offer Clear Alternatives to Negative Behaviors 86

Implement Incentives That Align With Needs 87

Work Together, and Have a School Plan 87

Summary 89

Reflection Questions 90

12 NO, OR QUID PRO QUO?
Negotiate With Students Who Are Struggling 91

Negotiation Starts With Common Ground 92

Strategies for Success 92

Use Reciprocity to Build Relationships 93

Establish Consistency 93

Use the Value of Social Validation 94

Motivate Through Scarcity 95

Summary. 96

Reflection Questions 97

13 THE UNINVOLVED PARENT
Reel Parents in With Three Basic Strategies 99

Strategies for Success. 100

Utilize Technology to Communicate 100

Offer Free Food and Childcare. .101

Think Like a Salesperson 101

Summary. 102

Reflection Questions *104*

14 STUDENT-LED CONFERENCES *with Mindy Crum*
Empower Students by Putting Them in Charge 105

A New Kind of Conference. 106

Strategies for Success. 106

Select and Announce Dates 107

Engage in Ongoing Communication 107

Gather Data. 108

Complete a Checklist 108

Conduct a Dress Rehearsal 109

Consider Your Room Configuration 110

Hold the Conference 111

Summary. 111

Reflection Questions *113*

PART 3

Owning It at Your School and District: Strategies for Succeeding
as a Member of a Staff Team 115

15 MAKING MEETINGS AN HOUR TO EMPOWER
Turn "Not Another Meeting!" Into "Let's Get to Business!". . .117

The Cultural Importance of Meetings 118

Strategies for Success. 118

Ask (and Answer) These Two Questions. 118

Reward Creative Thought 119

Invite Guests From Time to Time 120

Turn Routines Into Traditions 120

Summary. 121

Reflection Questions *122*

16 WELCOME TO TEACHING. PLEASE STAY
Help Your School's New Teachers Succeed (and Stick Around) 123
Strategies for Success. 124
Minimize Negative Talk 124
Celebrate Milestones and Successes .125
Include New Teachers in Decision Making (But Don't Force It). . .125
Help New Teachers Stay Healthy 126
Summary. 127
Reflection Questions 128

17 TALKING 'BOUT MY GENERATION
Improve Schools by Minding Collegial Generation Gaps . . .129
Generational Gaps and the Importance of Talking About Them . 130
Strategies for Success. 132
Acknowledge and Celebrate Generational Differences Openly.132
Create Teams, Mentorships, and Communications That Mind the Gaps 133
Remember the Common Goal 133
Summary. 134
Reflection Questions 135

18 WE NEED TO TALK
Approach a Colleague About a Conflict 137
How to Rethink Your Approach to Conflict 137
Strategies for Success. 139
Be Well-Rounded 139
Confirm Behavior Without Publicly Criticizing. 139
Make an Appointment 140
Rehearse and Open With Confidence 141
Be Specific. 141
Be Real and Listen 142
Make a Plan 142
Appreciate and Follow Up. 143
Summary. 143
Reflection Questions 144

19 TURN JOB SHARES INTO WIN-WIN-WINS *with Megan Pincus-Kajitani*
Learn Five Ways to Make Shared Positions Work for Teachers, Students, and Administrators 145
Strategies for Success. 146
Plan in Advance 146

Drop the Attitude 147

Begin and End the Year Together 148

Put It in Writing. 148

Set (Flexible) Limits 149

Summary 150

Reflection Questions *151*

PART 4

Owning It in Your Community: Strategies for Making a Positive Impact Beyond Your School and Classroom

. . . . 153

20 THE GENERAL PUBLIC ON TEACHERS
Turn Potential Foes Into Supportive Allies 155

All People Have Opinions—About Everything 156

Strategies for Success. 156

Stop Reading the News, and Start Creating It 156

Tell Stories 157

Offer Your Podium 158

Look the Part. 158

Brag Equally 159

Summary 160

Reflection Questions *161*

21 START SPREADING THE NEWS
Put the Spotlight on Your School. 163

We *Are* the Marketing Department 164

Strategies for Success. 164

Offer Campus Tours 165

Create a High-Quality Website 165

Find Your Niche and Brand It 166

Empower Student Voices 166

Summary 167

Reflection Questions 168

22 COMMUNITY-BASED PROFESSIONAL DEVELOPMENT
Get Teachers Into the Community and the Community Into Teachers. 169

The Purpose of Community-Based Professional Development . . .171

Strategies for Success. 171

Select a Topic and a Presenter 172

Find a Location. 172

Publicize It as an Experience, Not as a Workshop. 172

Plan Ahead. 173

Remind Everyone of the Intent. 173

Follow Up and Build Community 174

Summary. 174

Reflection Questions *176*

23 TEACHING TEACHERS
Step Up and Share Your Ideas With Fellow Educators

Step Up and Share Your Ideas With Fellow Educators 177

The Importance of Sharing Your Knowledge. 178

Strategies for Success—How to Get the Gig 178

Pick Your Topic 178

Write Your Blurb 179

Make Your Pitch 179

Be Easy. 180

Strategies for Success—What to Do Once You've Got the Gig. . . 180

Be Prepared and Flexible 180

Go Early 181

Learn by Doing 181

Tell Stories and Connect the Dots 182

Have Fun 182

Summary. 182

Reflection Questions *183*

24 THE 5-5-5 OF TEACHER BLOGS
Use Blogs to Learn, Share, and Influence Others

Use Blogs to Learn, Share, and Influence Others 185

Strategies for Success. 186

Five Reasons Blogs Are Important. 186

Five Blogs You Should Be Reading 187

Five Steps to Start Your Own Blog 189

Summary. 191

Reflection Questions *192*

Epilogue **193**

References & Resources. **195**

Index **203**

ABOUT THE AUTHOR

 **Alex Kajitani** is the 2009 California Teacher of the Year and a top-four finalist for National Teacher of the Year. He speaks nationally on a variety of education and leadership issues and delivers powerful keynote speeches and workshops to educators and business leaders. Also known as "The Rappin' Mathematician," Alex is on a mission to make sure *all* students master their times tables so they can be successful in mathematics and life. Thus, he created the first-of-its-kind, interactive, online times tables training program (www.MultiplicationNation.com).

Alex is the coauthor of *Chicken Soup for the Soul: Inspiration for Teachers*, has a popular TEDx Talk, and has been featured in many media stories, including *The CBS Evening News*, where Katie Couric declared, "I *love* that guy!"

To learn more about Alex's work, visit www.AlexKajitani.com.

To book Alex Kajitani for professional development, contact Solution Tree at pd@SolutionTree.com.

About the Contributors

Mindy Crum Hall is a fourth-grade teacher at a Title I school in North San Diego County, where the majority of her students are second-language learners who live in shared housing. Mindy has taught first through fifth graders since 2000.

Pete Fisher is a former behavior specialist and the 2006 Teacher of the Year for Escondido Union School District in California. He is a five-year standing cadre member of Southern California's Positive Environment of Network Trainers (PENT) and a trainer of Crisis De-escalation and Crisis Control.

Megan Pincus Kajitani is a professional writer, editor, educator, and former university career counselor. Her writing has been published in books, magazines, and newspapers, and she served as a career columnist for *The Chronicle of Higher Education* and *Inside Higher Ed*.

To learn more about Megan's work, visit www.mpk-ink.com.

FOREWORD

by Harry K. Wong

I remember the first time I met Alex Kajitani. I had just finished speaking at a conference when he approached me and introduced himself as a new teacher in a struggling, inner-city school. We chatted a bit, and he thanked me for my work. Before turning to leave, he handed me a CD filled with rap songs he'd created that he said were helping his students learn the mathematics lessons he was teaching.

Given that I'm more of a Broadway musical type, it took at least a week before those rap songs made it out of my bag and into my stereo. But from the first beat, I realized that what Alex had created was much more than a collection of songs. He had created a *solution*—a solution that got his students engaged, gave them the skills they needed to learn the concepts he was teaching, and motivated them to come back the next day. Moreover, he had created something that other teachers could use to do the same.

Quite simply, Alex was *owning* the challenge of engaging his students where they lived, while teaching them academic content they would use in their future lives. Instead of turning away from his struggles (and his students' struggles), Alex embraced them. He tried and found ideas that worked and put them in a format that other teachers also could use to be highly effective.

That's what this book is as well. No jargon. No fads. Instead, every chapter contains straightforward *solutions*, which you can use immediately, at no cost, to enhance your success as an educator. *Owning It* offers the kind of real answers that real teachers seek, for all the roles they play—from working with students in the classroom, to interacting with colleagues in staff meetings, to representing this crucial profession in the community.

Since writing *The First Days of School*, I've spent my career highlighting the work of highly effective teachers who provide well-managed, safe learning environments in which students thrive. I've followed Alex as one of these teachers. No longer a new teacher, he has grown to represent a new generation of education leaders who are using innovative, yet commonsense strategies to push the boundaries of what is possible for our students, our schools, and our profession.

Authentic, creative, and, above all, effective, I hope you find this book as relatable and real as Alex himself. I hope it stays on your desk as a resource that you return to as often as necessary. And I hope the solutions in these pages help you on your path to truly *owning it* as a teacher.

INTRODUCTION

There's this myth in teaching. This myth says you will struggle in your first few years but that, by your fourth or fifth year, you'll be experienced, things will be easy, and you'll have your act together. The truth is, while some years are better than others, teaching is hard *every* year, and every year, as teachers, we are asked to do more and more.

We live in a time of what some theorists call "accelerating change"—with exponentially faster technological, cultural, social, and environmental change than any other period in the known history of our planet (Kurzweil, 2001). We feel the effects of this firsthand in our schools and in our profession.

Each year, the group of students that enters our classrooms is vastly different from the group a year before. These students come with strong, evolving influences, from the latest technology to the year's newest hit television (or internet) show. Primarily, they come already equipped with new ways of thinking and operating in society.

Yet, as teachers, it is still our responsibility to ensure that they learn the academic content that someone else has deemed they learn, along with noncurricular life skills. It is also our responsibility to work with one another to help these students learn, which means we have to master grown-up communication and collaboration skills. Finally, it's our responsibility to represent our profession—and our schools and districts, and even our nation's educational system—to the wider community (the public) via all of the ever-changing modes of communication available to us.

Being a teacher is a multiskill, multifaceted, multipurpose role, a role that doesn't end when the bell rings, rather one we embody in our classrooms, in our schools, and throughout our communities. Thus, the great, challenging, overwhelming, enlightening, and rewarding responsibility it is to be a modern-day teacher.

Let's *own* this great challenge and responsibility—this great *opportunity* to make a difference.

What This Book Is

Whether this is your first year or your thirty-first year, this is a book that any teacher, of any age or subject, can use to address the many challenges we face each day. Every challenge this book addresses is one that I, and the many colleagues I've worked with over the years, have faced. Every strategy I list is one that I've used, refined, and taught to others.

I mean for this book to help you identify the root causes of many of the challenges we face as educators, give you easy-to-implement strategies for success that work, and ignite the best in yourself and your students. In short, I mean for it to help you be a highly effective teacher who *loves* what you do.

You may notice a running theme permeates this book's chapters, and that is the idea that whether we are talking about students, teachers, or members of the community, people are not fixed. We all have enormous capacity to learn and grow. Carol S. Dweck (2006) refers to this capacity as a *growth mindset*. In this spirit of growth mindsets, if you are a new teacher, then I'm excited for you to try some of these strategies, and I assure you—they are powerful. If you've been teaching for a while, some of these strategies will still be new to you, while others may not be. The reason they're included in this book is because I and other teachers have used them, and *they work*. Even if you already have experiences with many of them, my goal is to give you a fresh perspective on *why* you are using them and how they can help you make an even bigger impact with your students and their learning.

This book is a compilation of columns that I originally wrote for the nonprofit organization Reaching At-Promise Students Association (RAPSA, https://rapsa.org). The columns became wildly popular among teachers, and for this book, I have thoroughly reviewed and updated them to go even deeper and reflect new changes and ideas that have come along since I first wrote them. Each column is both an exploration of our many roles as teachers and a quick-reference handbook of strategies you can pull out in many of the situations you are likely to find yourself in daily in your classroom, school, and community.

This is a book that will help teachers feel more prepared for our increasingly multifaceted roles, and a book that will inspire teachers—like you—to remember why you entered this greatest profession and what incredibly important work you do every day.

It's a book about *owning it*—stepping up to and embracing our myriad roles as modern teachers and acing each one—for the benefit of our students, our schools, our communities, our profession, and even our nation.

Whether you are a teacher, a coach, or a mentor, my goal is to make this a book you can pick up and leaf through, and find something useful to implement in your work and life *immediately*, along with some validation about how amazing you are, juggling all of the roles we teachers fill in a fast-changing era.

How This Book Is Structured

Lots of teaching books focus on our role in the classroom, and so does this one. But this book does something else I've not found in the many teaching books I read: it focuses on our roles as classroom leaders, as mentors to challenging students and students who are at risk, as colleagues and members of a staff team, *and* on our roles as public professionals, representing our profession throughout the wider community. To that end, I divided this book into four parts, each one focusing on one of these roles. Excelling in all of these roles is critical in our profession.

Part 1: Owning It in Your Classroom

Part 1 (chapters 1–7) provides easy-to-implement, specific strategies that *all teachers* can use to connect with, engage, and ensure learning for all students.

Each year in the classroom, I have students in my class who, despite living in dire poverty, perform at the top of the chart on state tests. Sitting next to them are students who could not read, tell time, or speak English. Yet my school and community expect me to teach them all and do so at a level that is challenging to each of them. That's why I devote the first part of this book to the role we play, not as teachers of a specific subject or level, but as *teachers of students* and as *classroom leaders* who are responsible for every kind of everyday learning, who are accountable to test scores and parents, and who are accountable to every student who crosses our doorway.

I share what I've learned on the ground in my classroom about such topics as how to increase our powerful presence in the classroom, how to use the first five minutes of class to set the tone, how to engage and encourage all students, and how to manage such realities of classroom teaching as standardized tests and data.

This part represents a valuable quick-reference guide for any teacher looking for a little burst of fresh air in his or her day-to-day teaching or for ways to handle the many challenging classroom situations all teachers face.

Part 2: Owning It With Your Most Challenging Students

Part 2 (chapters 8–14) focuses on those few students who seem to demand more attention and discipline than the rest of the class combined. Known widely as the

Pareto Principle, 20 percent of our collective students often seem to provide 80 percent of our classroom challenges ("Guru: Joseph Juran," 2009). They are the students who are most challenging to connect with, to keep on task, and to help perform academically. They are the students who frustrate us, often to the point of exasperation.

They are also the students who need us the most. They are the students whose parents may not seem deeply committed to their education or were, themselves, unsuccessful in school. They are the students who fall into the so-called "achievement gap," and often are lost in there (Auguste, Hancock, & Laboissiere, 2009).

That's why I devote these chapters specifically to the ever-important role we play as teachers of students who are struggling or are at risk of dropping out of school. In this part, I offer strategies on topics such as connecting with students at risk, negotiating with them, honoring their cultural backgrounds, involving their parents, and empowering them to have a stake in their own education.

Part 3: Owning It at Your School and District

I devote part 3 (chapters 15–19) to the role we play as colleagues—both in our schools and within our districts or organizations. The days of the one-room schoolhouse are long gone, and working with a group of colleagues is an essential part of being a teacher. Just as we teach a group of students with a wide range of abilities and experiences, the teachers and administrators we work with are vastly different in their experiences, knowledge, and philosophies.

We're not all teachers for the same reason, yet we're all expected to do the same job. With over 17 percent of our colleagues leaving this job within the first five years (National Center for Educational Statistics, 2015), it's time for all of us to *own* the fact that, as educators, we are truly dependent on each other. That's why the chapters in part 3 provide practical and real strategies you can use to *incorporate, not eliminate* our differences, and draw upon each other's strengths.

It may seem, at times, that the issues and challenges I call out in these chapters have traditionally been the responsibility of principals and district administrators to address. However, owning it as teachers means stepping forward and utilizing creative, collaborative solutions that are practical and effective for the work that we do each day.

Offering strategies ranging from coming up with creative ideas for staff meetings, to addressing the generation gaps (yes, gaps!) between teachers, to strategizing for how to approach a colleague to have a difficult conversation, I based this part on the belief that the number-one factor in the success or failure of a school is the relation-ships of the adults in the building.

Part 4: Owning It in Your Community

I devote part 4 (chapters 20–24) to the role that we play as public professionals, representing our schools, our students, and the whole convoluted concept of educa-tion. Teaching is not just what we do. *Teaching is what we are.* It doesn't end when the last bell rings or when vacation starts. The time has come to *own* this role too.

As a profession, we often feel under attack from lawmakers, parent groups, and the general public, so many of whom buy into the idea that our education system is failing and that the solution is to simply "fire all the bad teachers." The strategies I offer in this part include how to positively represent our schools and our profession in the public eye, how to utilize various media to do so, and how to step up and become a teacher leader by sharing what you know, not just with colleagues at your school, but also at regional, state, and national conferences. When teachers lead, we elevate our profession, and everyone wins.

How to Use This Book

This book is like the friend that you go to when you just need some straightforward answers. I mean for you to read it easily and efficiently, and I designed every strategy to be immediately implementable with little to no cost to you.

You don't need to read this book from cover to cover (though I hope you will!). You can leave this book near your desk or nightstand and pull it out to read just one section on an issue you're dealing with at the moment or to get a little jolt of motivation on a hard day. I also hope you will consider reading it as a group with your school or district staff teams and work on the strategies together. In fact, that's precisely why I included a section for reflection questions at the end of each chapter. Use these to reflect on your own teaching practices and stir the pot for discussion with your colleagues.

In the end, use this book however it works for you, to inspire yourself to own it by owning your complex and expanding role in the most important profession during one of the most rapidly changing times in history.

Let's *own it* together and show the world that the future of education is brighter than some may think, with teachers like us taking the lead in our classrooms, our schools, and our communities.

PART 1

Owning It in Your Classroom: Strategies for Creating an Environment of Achievement

TIME TO GET REAL

Revisit Your Personal Philosophy's Value

A component of teaching I think is important for every educator is having a personal philosophy or some core beliefs that underpin how you view your role as a teacher. If you are just beginning your teaching journey, this might be something new for you, or at least something not yet fully formed. If you have many years or decades of teaching behind you, this is something you can easily articulate. Regardless, allow me to take you back to the days when I was training to become a teacher.

When I enrolled in a credential program in 2001, my first assignment was a two-page essay on my philosophy of teaching. A year later, at the end of the program, the director told us that the first question a job interviewer would ask us would be, "What is your philosophy of teaching?" Although no interviewer actually asked me that question during interviews, I always saw its importance for teachers new and seasoned. It makes us think about what we do and why, and it holds us accountable.

After more than ten years on the job, having worked with countless students and having experienced all of the challenges, rewards, thinking, and rethinking we associate with teaching, I have finally pieced together enough information to truly answer that first important question. My philosophy can be summarized in two words: *be real*.

In this chapter, I want to share this philosophy with you, as a motivation to start off a new teaching year or semester, as a reminder for myself, and as a call to reconsider (or consider for the first time) your own teaching philosophy in action. Using the strategies I provide, you can adapt and use my philosophy as you see fit. As fellow teachers in the trenches, I think it will resonate with you.

What It Means to Be Real

Be real means be real with yourself and be real with your students. Teaching is an art, a science, a passion, and an opportunity. It is an opportunity to prepare students not only for the world as it is but for the world *as it can be*. It's an opportunity to summon the past, to examine the present, and to shape the future.

Real teaching is not perfect teaching, and real teachers are not flawless people. We have moments where we stumble, and entire days we'd rather forget. Students and colleagues say things to us (sometimes good, sometimes not so good) that will forever imprint on our soul. Yet we allow those moments, and those days, to become a part of who we are, to strengthen us, and to keep moving forward. When we *own it*, we're being real.

True teaching takes courage. It takes persistence. It takes honest self-reflection in order to continuously improve. It requires being real with oneself about what is necessary to be a great teacher.

Strategies for Success

My philosophy for being real includes three core strategies: (1) teach what is real, (2) be reliable (or be *realiable*, if you prefer), and (3) be realistic. I detail each of these strategies in the following three sections. You can use or adapt them as best suits your own teaching philosophy.

Teach What Is Real

No student can truly learn a subject, especially the mathematics that I teach, if he or she does not see the relevance of the information in his or her everyday life. To help build connections between the content I teach and students' own interests, I constantly look for ways I can meet them where they live. On any given day, I weave lessons about the mathematics the students are learning with issues important to them, such as advertising, the internet, and popular music. I make it my mission to never have students leave my class thinking that they will not use the information we discussed or wondering how that information relates to the world around them.

I'll never forget when one of my students told me how she had been looking at a bridge and noticed all of its parallel lines, a subject I had covered in class. It occurred to me the student would never see bridges (or parallel lines) the same again, and when students see how the content we teach fits in to the context of their lives, that's teaching what is real.

Be Reliable

Put simply, we cannot demand that our students be organized, focused, and passionate unless we ourselves are all of these. With each word we speak, each lesson we deliver, and each situation we react to, we're teaching our students *who we are.* When we present ourselves as adults whom students can rely on, we have every right to ask our students to be reliable as well.

As an example, my students know what is expected of them well before they enter my classroom each day. My expectations of them, the procedures in my classroom, and my relaxed yet firm and consistent manner are all aspects of my teaching that my students can rely on. In cases where students make poor choices, and consequences are clear and necessary, I've found they often readily accept those consequences because I've delivered them with consistency and fairness. As I embody the traits of a reliable human being, my students learn what it takes to be reliable human beings.

Be Realistic

Living in one of San Diego's poorest neighborhoods, my students are constantly dealing with serious issues of violence, racism, and low literacy rates (to name just a few). It is not realistic for me to expect each of my students to show up on the first day proficient in his or her academic content areas. However, throughout the year, I take students from where they are to where they can be.

In this book's introduction (see page 2), I wrote about the importance of establishing or building in students a growth mindset (Dweck, 2006). I believe all students in my class can learn, can improve, and can surpass their own expectations of themselves, regardless of where those expectations previously began and ended. I also believe this is true of every student in every classroom. Perhaps not every one of your students will graduate from college; however, each and every one of them will someday be a neighbor, a coworker, and a person who has the potential to make a better world for those around them and those who come after them.

Summary

Educating is hard. I believe, and most teachers I know agree, educating struggling students is arguably the hardest job there is. However, it is my philosophy that, as teachers, we are working *for* those with the most potential to create a brighter future for everyone. This is why I teach, and this is why I *love* teaching. Being real with your students is an opportunity to engage in real teaching while teaching what is real.

Here's to getting real and getting to the heart of being teachers.

Reflection Questions

Now that you have completed the chapter, consider and reflect on the following questions.

1. In a few sentences, what is *your* philosophy of teaching?

2. How has your philosophy changed (or stayed the same) since you first began teaching?

3. As an educator, what do you still yearn for?

4. How might you change your instructional approach to be more real with your students? How might your students benefit from such a change?

FIRST IMPRESSIONS
Make the Most of the First Five Minutes of Any Class

Remember the old Head & Shoulders shampoo tagline? *You never get a second chance to make a first impression.*

As teachers, we actually get a chance to make a first impression *every single day*—often several times per day with each class we teach. With students who are accustomed to the rapidly paced sound bites and topic switches of a new media world, if we don't grab their attention quickly, we know that they often tune us out and the rest of the class period is usually shot. That's why the first five minutes of any class are crucial: they are an opportunity to connect with students, set the tone, convey expectations, and state in clear terms that day's goals. In this chapter, I establish how students are your customers and then detail five strategies you can use to make the most of your first impression every day and with every class.

Students Are Your Customers

Before I was a teacher, I managed a seafood restaurant on the California coast. There, I learned many valuable lessons about the impact of first impressions, making connections, and retaining customers. Although our students can't easily walk out and choose another place to go to school if we don't quickly meet their needs for connection, engagement, quality, and comfort (as restaurant customers are apt to do), our students can certainly choose to not participate if those needs are not met—and then everyone loses.

As educator Lee Watanabe-Crockett (2019) writes, "In order to learn something, it must stimulate your curiosity—in other words, interest comes before learning does" (p. 21). The research of Mary Helen Immordino-Yang corroborates this in her studies on brain function: "When students are emotionally engaged, we see activations all around the cortex, in regions involved in cognition, memory and meaning-making, and even all the way down into the brain stem" (as cited in Lahey, 2016).

Strategies for Success

If you lose your students' attention and focus within the first five minutes of class, it's pretty tough to restore it once you dive into the deeper end of the day's learning. Here are five critical steps—from this former restaurant manager turned teacher— toward making the first five minutes of your class both engaging and effective.

Connect Quickly

Have you ever walked into a restaurant and stood inside the door with a blank look on your face, waiting for the host or hostess to come and greet you—but the staff just whizzed around you, not acknowledging that you were there? Think about the stark contrast of this to the restaurant where someone greets you promptly at the door, warmly welcomes you, and has water and bread at the table as you're getting comfortable.

Perhaps warm bread isn't a part of our pedagogy, but good customer service should be. When we greet and acknowledge our students as they enter our classrooms, we make them feel welcome, relaxed, and happier to be there. Obviously, there are times when greeting each student by name is not possible; however, eye contact, an affirming nod, or a thumbs-up is often enough connection for our students to feel noticed and welcome. This means they are also more open to learning. When looking more deeply into this, R. Allan Allday and Kerri Pakurar (2017) find that when the teacher greets "problem" students at the door, student engagement increases from 45 percent to 72 percent at the start of class. In addition, and as I write in chapter 3 (page 24, Greet Your Students at the Door), it firmly sets the tone that, as the teacher, you are well-prepared, in charge, and happy to be there.

Lose the Lull

Continuing with the restaurant analogy, when the tables are full and patrons must wait, what do smart restaurants have them do? *Preview the menu.* Reading the menu, seeing the daily specials, planning a drink order, and so on get us thinking about the foods ahead of us. This keeps us from getting bored and irritated, gives us time to process and ask questions, and eliminates confusion. By the time we are seated at a table, we are usually hungry, decisive, and ready to order.

As our students sit down at their desks, they should never have to ask, "Now what?" On the very first day of school, I train my students that each day they should look for a warm-up activity on display when they enter my classroom. They also know I expect them to be working on it *before* the bell rings. Of course, if they need to take a breath or take care of something before that bell, I make sure to be understanding of that, but they need to be working when that bell rings. As Harry Wong and Rosemary Wong (2014) write in *The Classroom Management Book*:

> Every minute of the school day needs to be used effectively. Students are more productive if they have an assignment to work on as soon as they step into the classroom each day. This sets the tone for the class period of the day—the students are there to work and learn. (p. 71)

Engaging students in a warm-up task also ensures they have already dealt with preparatory routines such as sharpening their pencils or turning on their devices. These kinds of things save you significant time during the first five minutes of class, keep students engaged, and eliminate the need to constantly remind them what they should be doing.

Grab Their Attention

Which do you prefer: a waiter who mumbles a monotone "Hello" and then rambles off the specials, bored and looking at the ceiling, or one who enthusiastically explains each dish in juicy detail, engages you in conversation, and throws in a joke or compliment?

Students, especially our struggling students (see part 2, page 59), need something more than just being lectured to. Consider engaging their minds *and* bodies with an opening clap. Say, "Welcome, everyone, let's start out with a two-clap on the count of three. Ready? One, two, three . . ." Or, perhaps tell a funny story that happened to you on the way home from school the previous day or over the weekend. You don't have to be a stand-up comedian with an opening monologue, but a quick joke, a short video clip, or an interesting news story that relates to what you are going to teach can all be excellent attention grabbers.

Provide Purpose

Why do you choose to eat in any particular establishment? Do you need filling comfort food; a light, quick meal; or something spicy and exotic? You always have a reason or purpose for what you choose to eat. Although students can't necessarily choose what they are going to learn on a given day, they can certainly understand whether what they are learning has a purpose or not.

Here are three steps for clearly communicating a lesson's purpose to students.

1. **Write it:** Have your objective clearly posted in the same, accessible place each day. Make sure it is in student-friendly language! For example:

   - *Objective—The students will be able to calculate measures of central tendency.* (Not student friendly)

   - *Objective—We will calculate mean, median, and mode, and be able to describe each to a friend.* (Student friendly)

2. **Say it:** In a straightforward manner, say to your students, "By the end of class today, you will be able to calculate mean, median, and mode. You'll know you can do this because you will be able to tell a friend how to do it, as well as do it by yourself when I'm not in the room." (This is most effective if you say this while pointing to it in the written form as in step 1.)

   Here is where you can also connect the lesson to a larger purpose in their lives by saying something like, "Believe it or not, you will use these skills when you are doing real things in your life, such as shopping for houses and negotiating salaries for a job."

3. **Ask for it back:** Make the students tell you why they're there. After completing steps 1 and 2, ask a student aloud: "Hey, Brandon, please tell us why we're here today."

When you take these three steps, you help your students see the purpose in what they will do at the beginning of each class. Establishing this connection is part of your job—*your students need to know why they're there.* As assessment experts Rick Stiggins, Judith A. Arter, Jan Chappuis, and Steve Chappuis (2004) state, "Explaining the intended learning in student-friendly terms at the outset of a lesson is the critical first step in helping students know where they are going" (p. 58).

Cut the Hypocrisy

Would you trust a server at a health-food restaurant who looks run down and out of shape? Or one at a five-star restaurant who dresses sloppily and speaks incorrectly? This isn't about cosmetic appearances. It's deeper. It's about authenticity. We can't truly sell what we don't truly embody.

Often, I see teachers chatting in the halls, texting, or running to or from the copy machine as the final bell rings. Admittedly, I've done all of these things as well. However, when we do, we severely weaken the power we have to insist that our students get to class on time, be ready to learn, and stay attuned to what we're asking them to do.

The key to our students being well-prepared, curious, and passionate human beings begins with us, as teachers, also displaying those characteristics. For me, the following paraphrased, oft-told story (Mehta, n.d.) perfectly illustrates our role as teachers:

> A troubled mother took her daughter to see Mohandas Gandhi, who was world-renowned for his great spiritual discipline. It seems the young girl had become addicted to eating sweets, and her mother wanted Gandhi to speak to her about this harmful habit and convince her to drop it. Upon hearing this request, Gandhi paused in silence and then told the mother, "Bring the girl back to me in three weeks and I will speak to her then."
>
> Just as she was instructed, the mother returned with her daughter, and Gandhi, as he had promised, spoke to the girl about the detrimental effects of eating too many sweets. He counseled her to give them up.
>
> The mother gratefully thanked Gandhi, but was perplexed. "Why," she asked him, "did you not speak to my daughter when we first came to you?"
>
> "My good woman," Gandhi replied, "three weeks ago, I myself was still addicted to sweets!"

Summary

The next time you step into your classroom, notice what you do in the first five minutes of your class to make an impression, think about how your choices and routines set the tone for student success or failure, and consider how some simple changes could reap huge benefits for you and your students. By serving your students some appetizing learning from the moment they walk in the door, you encourage them to be focused throughout the session!

Reflection Questions

Now that you have completed the chapter, consider and reflect on the following questions.

1. Why is it important to see your students as your customers? How does this outlook help you better serve your students' interests?

2. What are the first three things your students should do *immediately* upon entering your classroom? Write them down, and then ask students to do the same thing. Are your answers the same?

3. What are some ways that you can grab your students' attention at the beginning of a lesson?

4. What's something that you do as a teacher but ask your students not to do? (Be honest with yourself!)

VISIBILITY IS EVERYTHING

Increase Your Classroom Presence to Seem Like You're Everywhere at Once

Every teacher with classroom experience knows that simply managing your classroom can be an everyday challenge that often overshadows instruction and learning. One of the keys to ensure your classroom stays on track is to create the impression that you are always visible and aware of what goes on within its walls.

When I was a new teacher, I really struggled. All the typical new-teacher clichés applied: my students were constantly off task, I shouted more "be quiet or else" warnings than I had time to enforce, and I left school each day feeling disrespected. Too often, I didn't feel my students learned anything that day. I found this frustrating because, in my credential program, I'd excelled in all of my teaching-theory classes and had been a pretty decent student teacher. But all of a sudden, on my own in a real classroom, I was sinking.

Then, my dad gave me a book that had seemingly nothing to do with teaching, yet it changed my teaching forever. *The Tipping Point* by Malcolm Gladwell (2002) outlines the work of two sociologists, James Wilson and George Kelling, and their *broken-windows theory*. In this chapter, I explain the thinking behind this theory and how it applies to education. I then present five strategies you can use to ensure there are no broken windows in your own classroom.

The Broken-Windows Theory

The broken-windows theory is quite simple. It's based on the contested belief that crime is the *inevitable result of disorder* (Kelling & Coles, 1996). Thus, if you walk by a building with a broken window (or several), you make the connection in your mind that *nobody cares for that building* and that, if you choose, you are free to go into the building and commit more (and more severe) crimes, with very little potential for punishment.

Gladwell (2002) paints the picture of New York City in 1990, when crime was at an all-time high, and twenty thousand felonies per year were being committed on the subway system alone (Kelling & Coles, 1996). Believing that the city's history of letting seemingly small, insignificant crimes go unpunished had created in peoples' minds the perception that they were free to commit more serious crimes, the mayor and police chief decided to implement the broken-windows theory. They ordered the police to crack down on two of the city's most visible crimes: graffiti and subway turnstile jumping.

Although they received much criticism for putting so much energy and so many resources into these smaller infractions, by 1996, felonies on the New York subway system had fallen by 75 percent, and murders dropped by 66 percent. To be fair, there were many factors at work, and there is justifiable debate regarding the correlation or causation regarding this policy and crime reduction; however, there is no question public perception changed from one of chaos to orderliness, and the health and productivity of the city improved (Gladwell, 2002).

So, as I read this book, I couldn't help but ask myself, "If application of the broken-windows theory could contribute to turning around one of the world's largest cities, how might it apply to my classroom?"

I adapted the theory to my role as an educator—not thinking of myself as a police officer, but more as a wise guide (think Yoda from *Star Wars*), and not thinking of students as criminals but as young people who, regardless of what past experience they bring to my classroom, can thrive with clear, firm guidance (think Luke Skywalker).

The next morning, I walked into my classroom, determined to change my students' perception of it. No longer would they view my class as an out-of-control environment where they were free to roam; rather, I needed to transform my class into a safe place they recognized as well-organized and effectively managed. I decided to focus hard on two smaller, but much more visible infractions (undesirable behaviors): chewing gum and arriving late to class. I announced to my classes that when we respect our classroom and its expectations, we respect ourselves and our learning.

So, starting at that moment, chewing gum or walking in late to class would result in an automatic detention. Then I held firm.

I devoted all my energy that day to noticing and acting on these admittedly two minor offenses. It was exhausting. The next day, I devoted about 50 percent of my time toward this, and the next, just a little. By the end of the week, my students were on task, following directions and, dare I say, learning. The following week, when I announced that I would be gone one day and that a substitute teacher would be taking my place, I overheard a student say, "I'm not misbehaving when the sub is here. Mr. Kajitani will bust you for gum—*just imagine* what he'll do if you act out for a sub!"

It was at that point that I realized a crucial truth: visibility is everything. Although assigning consequences and holding students accountable are necessary components of any classroom, intentional, well-thought-out expectations and clear, consistent rules are what truly set the tone and foster a positive classroom culture. Award-winning educator Tom Hierck (2017) writes in *Seven Keys to a Positive Learning Environment in Your Classroom*:

> *Expectations* serve as guidelines that are important not only in the classroom but, more often than not, also in life beyond the classroom's four walls. Expectations guide student responses academically and behaviorally. Expectations have an emphasis on lifelong learning and an eye toward growth. *Rules*, on the other hand, tend to be specific and are often responses to previous negative outcomes. *Rules* are attempts to guide student responses, but tend to be reactionary and often do not bring about the desired change. (p. 20)

There are all sorts of reasons that students act out, and I write about many of them in part 2 (page 59), but when it comes to general classroom management, our students' *perception* of what is happening in our classrooms determines how they *act* while in our classrooms. Like with the Force, the true power lies in students' minds.

Strategies for Success

There are a variety of ways you can model for your students to set a tone of positive expectation. The tips in the following five sections can help you increase your powerful presence in the classroom, while keeping your students focused on the learning at hand.

Make Phone Calls Home

Before the first day of school starts, I call the home of every one of my students. (It takes a while, but the time I save not dealing with discipline issues throughout the year comes back tenfold.) I ask to speak with the students themselves, and I tell them that I will be their mathematics teacher that year, that I need them to be in their seat in Room 12 before the bell rings, that they need to have a pencil and paper each day, and that chewing gum is absolutely prohibited. Of course, the specifics that apply best to your school culture and classroom environment may vary from what I list here. Perhaps your students all use tablets or laptops rather than pen and paper. The point is, before they even set foot on campus, you have created the perception you are firm, organized, and paying attention. Keep the conversation short and sweet, and save lengthier discussions about class policies for when your students are all in class together.

Honk and Wave While Driving to School

Each morning, as I drive through my school's neighborhood, I often see my students walking along the sidewalks. I always honk and wave to them as I drive past. Not too excitedly, but just enough to send them the message that my classroom extends far beyond its walls, and I'm looking out for them at all times. Would-be ditchers always have to reconsider, as they know I've already seen them and will expect them in my class. As I walk onto campus, I always say a pleasant "good morning" to every student I walk by, just to remind them that I see them, wherever they are, and that I'm excited to have them in class.

One of my best friends is a successful real estate developer. He makes it a point to attend every networking event in the area. He says, "The reason I go is not just to meet new people, but I want everyone in the business to know that if they cheat me on a commission, they're going to have to see me everywhere they go." Needless to say, very few people have ever tried to take advantage of him. Although our intent is for their benefit and not our own, we send the same message to our students every time we greet them outside of our classrooms.

Greet Your Students at the Door

Nothing says, "I'm paying attention" more than your initial contact with your students as they enter your classroom. As you greet them, insist on eye contact. Take the time to speak with your students about the importance of eye contact in our culture. Practice it, insist on it, and enjoy its benefits by using that connection to get to know your students as individuals while letting them also get to know you. Visibility works both ways, a theme you will see return in several of the strategies in part 2.

Utilize the Eyes in the Back of Your Head

No teacher has eyes in the back of his or her head, but there are ways you can give your students the impression that you do. One of my absolute favorite classroom-management tricks often works in something resembling the following three steps.

1. You see that two of your students (we'll call them David and Ben) are off task. Instead of immediately correcting them, *remain silent.*

2. Walk to the opposite side of the room and begin helping another student. With your back completely turned, say loudly, "David and Ben, please stop talking and finish your work." Never look up or make eye contact with David or Ben. Continue helping the original student.

3. David and Ben will be shocked and will wonder how you knew they were talking. (That's some Yoda magic right there.) While elementary school students will marvel at your seemingly magical skills, even secondary school students won't be able to deny your innate ability to know what's happening at all times.

This trick is effective while you are working at the board or sitting at your desk. Each time, continue about your business as if it's a regular part of your teaching. Again, you've created the perception that you are everywhere all at once, and affirmed that as teachers, visibility is everything. Of course, use your best judgment when dealing with more severe cases of discipline, but the more you can put a stop to disruptive behavior without having to engage in threats or consequences, the better.

Insist on a Clean Floor

One minute before class ends, I announce to my students, "This floor was spotless when you walked in; it needs to be spotless as you walk out." Because the point of this exercise is about having respect for the learning environment, I train the students to pick up any trash around the vicinity of their desks, regardless of whether they are responsible for it being there. This reinforces the impression that everything that is happening in my classroom is visible and that everyone in the classroom is accountable. It also sets up the next class for success as students enter.

Summary

Just as the broken-windows theory contributed to cleaning up New York City, it can also restore and promote a positive learning space for your students to do their best work. You just have to identify those core and most visible behaviors that tend to lead to increased disruption and then be willing to be firm and consistent in addressing those behaviors. What are they? Name them, eliminate them, and get back to teaching those young Jedi who need us.

Reflection Questions

Now that you have completed the chapter, consider and reflect on the following questions.

1. What are the two most visible offenses that occur in your classroom? How do they impact you, your instruction, and other students? What could you start doing tomorrow that would decrease these behaviors?

2. Which of the strategies listed in this chapter could you start using right *now*, and what effect do you hope it will have?

3. Consider the methods you use to address classroom disruptions. Do the strategies you use promote positive student behavior without resorting to arbitrary consequences? How might you alter your approach to incentivize positive behavior in a more productive way?

4. Which teachers at your school are known for having the best classroom-management skills? Consider setting up a time to go and watch them in action! Then, try a few of their techniques in your classroom and see what happens.

PLEASE STOP THINKING
Understand Four Things Teachers Say That Sabotage Learning

As teachers, we always keep an eye out for the teachable moment, those unexpected twists and turns (usually student-prompted) in our daily routine that allow us to grab hold of a question or comment on a mistake and spark in our students knowledge that is real-time and interesting (Lewis, 2017). I've found that capitalizing on that teachable moment can often be the most memorable, powerful part of the day.

I find the challenge with making teachable moments memorable and powerful is that we disrupt students' ability to absorb that knowledge if we use words, phrases, and instructions that do *the exact opposite* of what we intend. Instead of invoking thinking, these words actually sabotage it. Bringing these phrases to our consciousness and then banning them from our teaching lexicon, using the strategies I present in this chapter, can help us truly take advantage of teachable moments and inspire learning in our classrooms.

Strategies for Success

Some successes depend on knowing what *not* to say. Here are four common variations of these teacher-spoken phrases, explanations for how students perceive them, and a few alternatives you can use instead that will keep your classes on track, on target, and ready for the next truly teachable moment.

Connect to What Students Do Know

Consider the following statements on learning.

- **What we say:** "You were supposed to have learned this last year."

- **What students hear:** "You didn't do what you were supposed to do last year, and it doesn't appear that you're doing it this year either."

These kinds of statements are problematic on multiple levels. In addition to being an implied put-down of the student, when we make this statement, we also imply that the teacher that they had last year didn't do his or her job properly. This creates a negative divide between you and the previous teacher as well as you and the student. In addition, often the student *did* learn it last year; they just don't recognize it now because it is in a different context with a different teacher.

Consider the following alternatives instead.

- "I believe you have *some* background knowledge about this concept. Tell me some of the things you know about _____."

- "Let's step back from this topic and look at some of the information we need to know in order to understand this." This is especially important for English learners because background knowledge is crucial for them to understand new material (Reyes, 2015).

- "Let me see a show of hands of who *does* remember this." (Some percentage of students will likely raise their hands.) "OK, those of you raising your hands have three minutes to pair up with those who do not and tell them everything you know about this topic."

All three of these statements take the responsibility of learning away from whatever happened (or did *not* happen) last year, and instead refocus the learning on the students, what they already know, and what they need to know. In addition, they do so in a way that is empowering for students.

Stress the Learning, Not the Testing

Consider the following statements on testing.

- **What we say:** "This is important. It will be on the test."

- **What students hear:** "Don't worry about all that other stuff. If I don't tell you it's on the test, it's not really something we need to focus on."

Tests, like grades, are important. But I've found that for most students, the best way to do well on tests and get good grades is to *learn*, *understand*, and *apply* the information. In addition, I've had several students over the years who show up with a history of poor grades, seemingly unmotivated by what will be on the test. Instead, they're motivated by knowing how the information you're teaching in class will help them in their lives. As teachers, one of our goals is to instill in our students a personal engagement in the subject we are teaching them.

This statement also undermines us as teachers. Placing the information's importance on the fact that it will be tested also sends the message that it is the only reason we're teaching it, that we are not in control of our curriculum, and that we ourselves do not understand its importance.

Consider the following alternatives instead.

- "This is important. It helps us understand the link between _____ and _____."
- "Tomorrow, we're going to study _____. Let's make sure we understand how _____ connects to _____, so that we can easily understand the connection when we uncover it tomorrow."
- "I didn't think that this was important when I learned it in school. But then, one day I _____." (Insert your own story here!)

All three of these examples take the emphasis off the test and promote the importance of a love of learning as well as lifelong learning. They help students make connections within the subject matter and connections between the information and their daily lives. When true learning happens, the test scores and grades often take care of themselves!

Remember That the One Doing the Talking Is Often the One Doing the Learning

Consider the following statements on talking during class.

- **What we say:** "Please stop talking."
- **What students hear:** "Please stop talking . . . and thinking!"

Yes, there are times when we need the students to stop talking so that we can give instructions. There are also times when personal issues are of greater interest to our students than our own teaching objectives for the day.

However, there are also times when the students *really are* talking about the subject matter. Consequently, when we demand that they stop talking, we are, many times, demanding that to be quiet, they switch from a brain filled with ideas and questions to one that is blank and uninterested.

Consider the following alternatives instead.

- "I am going to count down from ten. In those ten seconds, I want you to read the objective on the board and be prepared to discuss it." This helps shift the students' focus to what they *will* be learning today, while promoting reading and the ability to speak about what they've just read.

- "If you can hear me, clap once." (Wait three seconds.) "If you can hear me, clap twice." Not only is this an active way to get students to come together, it also helps build a "we're all in this together" classroom culture. It feels so good when everyone claps twice that second time! (This also promotes kinesthetics.)

- "When you hear me ring a bell, please bring your conversation to a close." Not only does the bell provide a sound different than your own voice, you can also offer a student the chance to ring the bell from time to time. It's a powerful moment for a student to see that he or she can bring the class to attention. If you can find a meditation bell with a very calming ring, these bells are especially good with older students. The goal, of course, is to have the class become quiet within a few seconds of you ringing the bell without you having to say anything at all.

- "As I lower my hand, change your conversations into a soft whisper. When I completely lower my hand, all conversation should cease." This one requires a bit of explanation in advance, but I have found students love the sense of participation it fosters. I liken it to how the end of a song fades into silence, as opposed to abruptly turning it off.

Students talk when they are excited. And in a nonstop world of texting and social networking, the floodgates seem always open for them to comment, reply, or like something. These are a continuous kind of talking in the online world, a world in which they're used to participating. The trick is to transition student talking into learning the subject at hand in a way that is smooth, effective, and engaging to the students while still respectful toward you.

Dig Deeper to Address the Issue Behind the Issue

Consider the following statements on not completing homework.

- **What we say:** "Why didn't you do your homework?"
- **What students hear:** "Quick: think of something to say to get the teacher off my back as soon as possible!"

Whether it's an age-old cliché ("The dog ate it" or "My brother ripped it") or a new-age cliché ("It didn't download" or "My printer ran out of ink"), we've heard them all. That said, it's important to keep in mind the reason we keep getting the same old answers is because we keep asking the same old question.

As famous sales guru Zig Ziglar (2002) says, "Failure is an event—not a person." When a student does not do his homework, focus on the act and the decision, not the individual or personality type. Treat failure to complete homework as a decision or as an event, and immediately move toward a solution-based approach.

Ask yourself the following questions.

- "Did the student record the homework assignment in class the previous day?"
- "Is the student required to care for younger siblings, and thus has little or no time to complete the work?"
- "Is the student leaving his or her homework until late in the evening when he or she is exhausted?"

I once had a student confess to me (after his fourth after-school detention for not doing homework) that he had lost his mathematics book. As soon as we got him a new book, the problem magically disappeared! Asking the right questions can help uncover the truth, as well as lead to some real solutions.

In their article "Strategic Questioning: Engaging People's Best Thinking," authors Juanita Brown, David Isaacs, Eric Vogt, and Nancy Margulies (2002) share this wisdom: "Leaders who ask, 'What's possible here, and who cares?' will have a much easier time gaining the collaboration and best thinking of their constituents than those who ask 'What's wrong here, and who is to blame?'" (p. 5).

Consider the following alternatives instead.

- "If you could relive yesterday, what would you do differently in order to get your homework done?"

- "If you could change one thing about where and when you do your homework, what would that one thing be?"

- "What are the biggest obstacles to you not getting your homework done?"

As teachers, we know that homework is the key to mastering concepts that we teach in class (often in a very limited amount of time). I often tell my students, "You haven't learned something until you can do it on your own, without my help."

Completing their homework is an essential part of this process. When we ask questions that focus on process and success, not failure, we can truly empower students to achieve inside and outside the classroom.

Summary

In sum, if we really want to seize those teachable moments with students, we must be willing to put ourselves in their shoes and examine our own vernacular for those phrases that sabotage their learning. Then, we must erase those phrases from our teaching vocabulary and redirect them into words that inspire and empower our students to think beyond what they've been hearing for years and instead engage in their own learning.

Reflection Questions

Now that you have completed the chapter, consider and reflect on the following questions.

1. What are some things you say that interfere with engaging students in a teachable moment? How might you change your words to more productively engage them?

2. Find an item that will be on your next test. What is the real, deeper reason that students need to learn it? How could you communicate this idea to them to stimulate their interest?

3. Have you tried any of the strategies mentioned for getting your students to quiet down? What is *your* most effective way to get your class silent, allowing you to begin speaking?

4. Name a student that hasn't turned in much homework recently. What could you say to this student to begin a conversation about finding the real, deeper reasons behind the missing homework?

I SAID BE QUIET . . . AND START TALKING

Help Students Learn Out Loud and Still Keep a Handle on Your Classroom

In chapter 4 (page 29), I wrote about ways your own words can disrupt teachable moments and achieve the exact opposite result of what you aimed for. This chapter also focuses on the power of words but focuses on ways to encourage your students to use their own voices, because one of the best ways to engage students is to make them active participants in their own learning.

I once had the opportunity to visit one of California's lowest-performing schools. Located in a high-poverty neighborhood, with test scores in the gutter, the school had all of the stereotypical low-performing attributes—except one. According to the school staff, there were very nearly *no* behavior or discipline problems.

As I toured from classroom to classroom, I had to agree. The students seemed very well-behaved, and the teachers seemed to have their procedures and routines down to a science. As bells rang, the students moved through the halls with grace and ease. Teachers didn't understand how they could work so hard all day without it reflecting in students' test scores.

As I continued to observe classrooms, I realized that the teachers absolutely were teaching. And that was the problem. The teachers spent so much time teaching, there was very little time left to devote to the students' *learning*.

By this, I mean I did not see time devoted to discussion and interaction between teachers and students, or between students and their peers. In a time when the four Cs (collaboration, communication, critical thinking, and creativity) are essential to success (Partnership for 21st Century Learning, 2015), the students' only learning option was to absorb lectures. How many of us learn best this way?

As veteran education consultant Sandi Novak and teacher Cara Slattery (2017) write about their work in establishing a framework for student-led discussions:

> [Students] will learn more, build their confidence, develop an appreciation of other perspectives, and improve their retention if they regularly converse with their peers. It also helps them refine or extend their repertoire of speaking and listening skills. Through discussion, students reflect on and assess their own learning, plan next steps, and *apply their learning in novel ways*—the ultimate learning goal. (p. 155)

In this chapter, I dive into the importance of making students participants in their own learning and follow that up with three strategies you can use to make their involvement more successful.

We Can't Fear Student Participation

With the rise of the internet, social media, and video-recording capabilities on every machine we can fit into our pockets, students are social beings by necessity. They are constantly talking, texting, and giving their opinions.

However, in schools, we often ask them to put all this aside and be quiet in order to "let the teacher teach." We often force students into roles in which they are expected to be quiet for an hour or more at a time, and then we expect them to remember everything we just said.

Many teachers are afraid that letting the students talk means risking giving up control of the classroom, and we fear that it will become difficult to reclaim that control in the middle of class. In their book *Checking for Understanding*, authors Douglas Fisher and Nancy Frey (2014) report that in classrooms with more low-performing or English-learning students, there is an even higher rate of teachers talking more and students talking less.

Giving into this fear of the messiness that may ensue when we engage students in interactive conversations is a disservice to them.

To ensure that our students learn the information we present to them, we need to give them time to *interact with* the information. This includes letting them discuss, question, and even argue and flub it while we act as observers, coaches, and facilitators to keep their learning on track while calling attention to their successes.

Strategies for Success

Letting students interact can appear messy. That's OK! Messy does not have to mean chaos. The following three strategies can help get students engaging with and discussing the curriculum they're learning—while allowing you to keep control of the classroom.

Use Think-Pair-Share

Developed by University of Maryland professor Frank Lyman (1981), the think-pair-share strategy encourages students to do exactly what the name suggests. Here's how it works.

Think

Begin by provoking your students to think about a concept or idea, or you can provide a specific question or prompt. Give the students a minute to think in silence. They can jot down notes about their thoughts as well.

One minute of think time is usually plenty; anything over a minute risks losing the momentum toward the outcome you desire. Giving this wait time also eliminates eager students shouting out their answers, which often becomes the only answer that the rest of the students then give. It also decreases the chances of a student hiding at his or her desk in hopes that you won't call on him or her.

Pair

Next, prompt students to turn to a partner (or partners) to discuss each student's individual thoughts or written notes. It is very important that you be visible during this time, either by circulating the room or sitting in on conversations that you believe may become unfocused. It is also a good idea to call out (sometimes quietly, other times as a class announcement) positive examples of students who are working well together.

You can add urgency to the conversations by giving students a time limit; for example, tell students, "You have one minute to discuss your thoughts with your partner." Of course, more complex topics, or higher-grade levels will require more than a minute! As students are discussing a topic, pay attention to voice tones and volume. These will often tell you when conversations have begun wrapping up.

In addition, it's helpful to have the students know who their partner is in advance of initiating this process. I like to mix things up with something as simple as having everyone in an odd-numbered row work with the person to his or her left or finding someone in the room with the same color eyes (still promoting that eye contact, as discussed on page 79, Understand and Honor Cultural Barriers). This helps the students stay focused on the conversation at hand and eliminates the potential for one student to sit alone quietly while the rest of the class engages in conversation.

As students share their answers, they do so in a situation that is much safer than saying it aloud for the first time in front of the entire class. Should they find that their answer is completely off base, they can quickly make the adjustment and have a better answer by the time the entire class discusses it. That said, more often than not, the students find that their answer *is* in line with what their partner was thinking, giving them confidence to move into the share phase.

Share

In the share phase, call for student pairs to share their discussion with the entire class. There are several options for having students share aloud, including the following.

- Call on those who offer to share.
- Call on all groups in a round-robin format.
- Call on individual students.

You can take the share process a step deeper by having students share only what their partner talked about. This ensures not only that students were talking to one another but that they were listening to each other as well. You can add further depth to the learning by recording (or having students record) key points from their discussions by documenting their work or using digital devices. This also provides a running record that students can access later to reinforce their learning.

Ask Three Questions

I designed the three-questions strategy, which my students enjoy referring to as "interrogator," to get students to break from the traditional precanned-questions format that is often found in textbooks or as mock job-interview questions. It helps them truly listen to their partner's response before moving on to the next question.

In addition, this strategy also compels students who are answering the questions to speak in a way that gives their partner enough depth and content to construct a new question. It works in two steps.

1. Have Student A ask Student B (his or her partner) three questions. As the teacher, you provide the first question for Student B to answer. (As students develop this skill, they can create their own first question.) Student A asks the second question but must build on his or her partner's answer to the first question. Student A then asks a third question, based on his or her partner's answer to his or her second question. Student A may *only* ask questions. Student B must provide *only* answers and must speak in full sentences. Although I've always done this as a verbal activity, you can implement it as a written activity or even have students use texting or other simple messenger-type formats.

2. Reverse the roles for the student pairs. Student B asks the questions, starting with the first one (teacher-provided), and Student A answers. You can increase the conversational rigor by not allowing Student B to ask the same questions that his or her partner already asked for the second and third questions.

Here's an example of how this conversation might look in an eleventh-grade English language arts class that is discussing *Walden* (Thoreau, 1854).

Student A (teacher-prompted): What does it mean when Thoreau says, "I would rather sit on a pumpkin and have it all to myself, than be crowded on a velvet cushion"?

Student B: I think it means that that it is better to have something that is cheap all to yourself, than to share something expensive with a lot of other people.

Student A: Have you ever had something that was cheap all to yourself?

Student B: When I was younger, my brother got a new bike, and I got his old one. Nobody asked me to try the old bike, but everyone wanted to try my brother's new bike.

Student A: If you had the choice, would you rather have had the old bike or the new bike?

Student B: Actually, my brother left the new bike at the park, and somebody took it. So, I guess Thoreau is right!

As leadership expert Simon Sinek (n.d.) says, "There is a difference between listening and waiting for your turn to speak." The three-questions activity helps students truly listen on a deeper level, and they usually get to know someone even better!

Record It

In my experience, there are many teachers who still fear technology in their classrooms. This is counterproductive to the world our students live in and must prepare for. When we demand that students put their phones away (while rolling our eyes), we actually neglect an extremely valuable tool to help them speak, especially our English learners. We also miss an opportunity to meet students where they live and help them engage with technology in a productive, educational way.

One way you can get students talking and learning while making use of their comfort with technology is to have them read or speak into their device—this helps them practice communicating in a way that is private and nonthreatening. Here are three activities you can have your students engage in to accomplish this.

1. Using technology such as smartphones or tablets, students can easily record themselves reading a passage and listen to it at their convenience as many times as necessary. They can then make adjustments to their reading, rerecord themselves, and hear the difference. Also, consider pairing up a weaker speaker with a stronger one so the weaker voice can hear a stronger voice read the same passage.

2. When you ask a question, have students record themselves speaking the answer. When called on, a reluctant speaker can simply hit Play for his or her partner or for the class to hear his or her prerecorded response.

3. Consider extending this activity by using a digital app, such as Sonic Pics (www.sonicpics.com), to have students record their voice over photographs and create a narrated slide show. Such apps are extremely easy to use, highly engaging for students, and very effective. An added benefit is that because students are recording their every word, they are much more likely to stick to the academic content that you insist on!

All three of these strategies benefit students tremendously by allowing them to be active participants in their own learning as they create, adjust as necessary, and create again; all while giving them an opportunity to produce something that gives them immediate feedback and might even be something they want to show off to others!

Summary

Although reading and writing are incredibly important to the success of our students, for many, the ability to speak well will help them not only achieve in school but throughout their lives. According to Harvey Mackay (2005), author of the book *Swim With the Sharks Without Being Eaten Alive*, the skill that is most lacking in business is public speaking, or the ability to present oneself.

Our students' ability to learn hinges on their ability to speak their minds and process their thoughts aloud. As authors Douglas Fisher, Nancy Frey, and Carol Rothenberg (2008) so eloquently note, "Oral language is the foundation of literacy." The ability to speak well allows students to present themselves in a confident manner in the world and gives them the potential to truly achieve the promise that we hold for them.

As teachers, we must have the courage to stop "teaching at" our students for hours on end and make the space for them to learn out loud, from their own voices, and from one another.

Reflection Questions

Now that you have completed the chapter, consider and reflect on the following questions.

1. Imagine you were successfully getting students to learn out loud in your classroom. What would this look and sound like?

2. Consider the think-pair-share strategy. What are some questions you could ask your students to focus on during an upcoming lesson?

3. Do you view your classroom as a place that provides many opportunities for students to discuss, share, and learn from each other? If so, what are some strategies you use for this? If not, what is holding you back? What strategies could you start implementing to increase student interaction?

4. Do you currently provide opportunities for your students to use their devices as learning tools? If so, good for you! If not, why not? Talk to some teachers who are incorporating personal technology into their classrooms. Ask them how they do it and what the benefits are.

DEAL WITH DATA

Transform Your Perception of Data and Help Your Students Succeed

For better or worse, data are the global currency for living in the 21st century world. We can either let data limit us and our students, or we can use data's power to our advantage and the benefit of our students. Consider this: What single factor ultimately determines whether a student is at risk?

It's not work ethic, as we all know students who don't like to work hard but are still skilled enough to make it through high school and even college. It's not ethnicity, as we all know students of different ethnicities who are low and high achievers. Nor is it gender, socioeconomics, or the neighborhood he or she lives in.

What ultimately determines whether a student classifies as at risk is the data we collect on him or her. Often, educators identify poor academic performance as a key indicator of students at risk of dropping out (Ormrod, 2010). Although different states have different names for students who meet, exceed, or do not meet standards, a student who consistently scores in the lowest category is indicative of a student at risk for dropping out of school. Within this label lies a multitude of complex factors such as work ethic, home life, and socioeconomics; however, it is often a student's *test data* that determines the label in official terms.

When I worked as a teacher on special assignment for my school district, administrators tasked me with helping our district actually use our masses of collected data to help students, teachers, administrators, and schools improve and succeed. For me, this task was nothing short of enlightening and inspiring, and my perceptions of data have shifted tremendously.

I now view data as having incredibly positive potential as a tool for our schools (as opposed to the darker side of data that puts us teachers on the constant defensive). As I went into schools each week and talked with fellow educators about how we could actually use all this data we collect—in big and small ways, in our classrooms and offices each day—I saw many of their perceptions begin to shift as well. In this chapter, I explain how we should define data and provide four strategies you can use to successfully utilize the data available to you in your own teaching.

How We Define Data

Businesses have always relied on sales data to reward and fire employees, project future earnings, and plan strategically. Politicians also rely on data, and many of them win or lose an election based on effective data use. In the 21st century, these practices have taken on even greater significance with sweeping implications and consequences for literally every person living in an internet-connected society ("The World's Most Valuable Resource Is No Longer Oil, but Data," 2017).

As an industry, education is just beginning to grasp the importance of analyzing data to help our schools and students achieve. However, most of the data-analysis methods we use are ones we learn on the job, as traditional credential programs often do not require data-analysis coursework as part of their requirements. This makes data an untapped resource with limitless potential to change the nature of learning, just as the Oakland As used data analysis to revolutionize baseball in the early 2000s (Lewis, 2003). (If you are unfamiliar, in 2002, the team's use of analytics helped it tie for the best record in Major League Baseball while having its third-lowest player payroll.)

First, it's important to understand what data are. Data, as defined by *Merriam-Webster's Online Dictionary*, are "factual information . . . used as a basis for reasoning, discussion or calculation" ("Data," n.d.). In other words, they are not limited to just numbers, and data on our students do not just come to us in the form of spreadsheets and statistics.

Data are information, and information educators can use to help students is the best kind. Thus, although test scores are the most talked-about form of data in

WATERS EDGE DERM- OKE
301 NE 19TH DRIVE
OKEECHOBEE, FL 34972

07/08/2022   07:45:16

CREDIT CARD

DISCVR SALE

Card #	XXXXXXXXXXXX9354
Chip Card:	Discover
AID:	A0000001523010
SEQ #:	1
Batch #:	1235
INVOICE	1
Approval Code:	008838
Entry Method:	Chip Read
Mode:	Issuer

SALE AMOUNT $80.00

CUSTOMER COPY

07.06.2022   07:45:18

CREDIT CARD

DISCVR SALE

Card   XXXXXXXXXX9951
Chip Card   Discover
AID   A0000001523013
Seq #   1
Ref #   1239
Invoice   1
Auth Code   00658
Entry Method: Chip Read
Mode   Issuer

SALE AMOUNT $80.00

education, we need not limit data collection to test scores. Think of data as any factual information that can help us reach students. For example, data can be any of the following.

- The number of times a student participates in class discussion in a given week

- Something a student says that indicates he or she is learning, such as, "The first time I took the test, I got 65 percent correct; the second time, I got 84 percent correct!"

- Your school's graduation rate

These examples, along with countless others, are real and valuable pieces of information teachers and administrators can use to demonstrate progress (or a lack of progress), understand the factors underpinning that progress (or lack thereof), and advocate for much-needed resources or celebrate achievement.

Strategies for Success

Ultimately, the tools at your disposal and your own imagination are the only limits on data's power to be a positive influence on how you teach and how your students most effectively learn. Here are four strategies you can use to effectively use data to better understand your students, respond to their needs, and direct them onto successful paths as quickly as possible.

Use Data to Begin a Conversation, Not to End It

As educators, we have an obligation to believe that all students can learn. Too often, we use data to justify why a student *can't learn*, as opposed to using them as a lens through which we can carefully plan instruction. Instead, use data to initiate the conversation rather than end it by changing your perception of what data communicate to you. Figure 6.1 (page 48) offers some examples of ways you can do this.

Although these examples may seem obvious in their nature, it is often too easy for us, as teachers under pressure, to make excuses for why our students aren't achieving, and then use data to back up our thoughts. This is a habit of mind worth breaking. Instead, use data to make statements and ask questions that lead to change and more positive outcomes.

As the End of a Conversation . . .	As the Beginning of a Conversation . . .
"Gerald is a far-below-basic student; he is going to have trouble completing this activity."	"Gerald scored far below basic on our last test; what strategies can I use to help him complete this activity?"
"Half of my class is currently reading below grade level. I doubt we'll be able to hit all of the state standards this year."	"With half of my class reading below grade level, I need to find ways to help them close the achievement gap, while at the same time challenge my students who are reading at grade level."
"Two-thirds of my students' parents never finished high school. They won't be able to help their children with their homework."	"Two-thirds of my students' parents never finished high school. What additional resources are available to help these students and help their parents to support them?"

Figure 6.1: Using data in a conversation.

See the Real Student Behind Every Piece of Data

One year when analyzing some test scores, I noticed that one of my students' scores had dropped significantly from his previous two test scores. I also noticed that he had not turned in some of his homework for the unit (something he usually did). When I presented him with the data, he confided that his parents were splitting up and that he hadn't been sleeping much over the past two weeks.

Although I was not well-informed on this student's life at home, because I was familiar with his data, I was able to quickly identify what he needed, and I arranged for him to meet with the counselor. The ensuing months were a challenge to keep him focused on his academics, something that would normally label him as at risk; however, because of the intervention and support he received, this student passed all his courses despite these challenges. This is an example of how thinking of a student as *at risk* is not as powerful as thinking of him or her as *at promise*.

When we accept the data as real, then we accept them as a useful component of our students' lives. While not every piece of data implies a life crisis, or a guaranteed success, it is important to remember that at the heart of all data is a real student with real struggles, hopes, and dreams. Combined, the data tell a story. As teachers, it is our job to identify and understand those stories and then use them to improve outcomes.

Make Data Useful by Not Keeping Them Secret

With so many school districts moving toward a value-added method of evaluating teachers—that is, seeking to identify how much of a positive or negative effect individual teachers have on students during the course of a normal school year—it is no surprise that many teachers are hesitant to share their data. It can be frightening! However, as educators, we must get past the stigma that so-called *bad data* automatically mean *bad teacher*.

Here's what I've learned: using data to truly help students succeed requires a group effort of teachers and administrators. We can't be afraid to admit when students are struggling despite our best efforts; rather, when we work within learning teams or any other collaborative climate that encourages open communication around data, we must take advantage of the opportunity. When you have students who scored low on a particular section of a test, identify fellow teachers whose students scored well and seek out their guidance and wisdom. Learning teams should make it standard practice to tap teachers whose students scored particularly well on a given portion so they can share their pedagogical practices and elevate the entire department's teaching practices.

Let's use data to identify areas of strengths and weakness in our individual students, as well as with our students overall, and choose as a profession to shift our perception of data as our enemy to that of another colleague working with us to help our students succeed. Each time we do this, our students will ultimately benefit the most.

Use Analogies to Make Data Friendly

The breadth and scope of data and the complex terminology involved in their analysis often gets scary, especially for those of us unfamiliar with data-analysis practices. It doesn't have to be that way. For example, I've discovered that many teachers find the achievement gap a difficult concept to grasp (Auguste, Hancock, & Laboissiere, 2009). A colleague of mine once described the achievement gap in a way that made everyone in the room understand it clearly. He said:

> Imagine all of the students except ours get in a big bus, and the bus takes off down the highway going sixty miles per hour. An hour later, our students get in a bus, which takes off going down the same highway, but at fifty miles per hour. Not only is that bus an hour behind, but at the rate it is going, our students will never catch up.
>
> The distance between the two buses is the achievement gap, and the only way to catch up to the first bus is to accelerate

the second bus, thus accelerating the learning. (Jason Hoff, personal communication, October 2011)

As everyone in the room nodded in agreement, it occurred to me my colleague had brilliantly used a simple analogy to explain something as complex as the achievement gap, to which so many of our at-risk students fall prey. (You can learn more about overcoming the achievement gap in chapter 8, page 61.)

Learning from this method, I used the following analogy to explain formative versus summative assessments:

> What's the difference between an autopsy and an MRI? (Long pause to give everyone in the room some think time.) Doctors use an autopsy after someone has died. They use it to answer the question, "What happened?" Although the results can be informative, there is no way to save the patient. All we can do is use the information we gain from the autopsy to help others in the future.
>
> This is similar to our end-of-year (summative) state assessments. We get the results, but by then, it is too late. The students have moved on to another grade, and we are quite limited in what we can do with the information.
>
> On the other hand, doctors use MRIs to identify areas of weakness. This allows them to act in a timely manner, prescribing a course of action for treatment to help a patient survive. In education terms, treatment means prescribing intervention strategies that will get our at-promise students on the right path before they drop out. This is effectively using formative assessment.

Sticking with the medical analogies, I also relate a trip to the doctor to taking these tests, as I tell my students:

> When you go to the doctor, the first thing they do is record your height and weight. That way, they can keep track of how much you have grown over the months and years. But your height and weight don't tell us everything, like how strong you are or how happy you are.
>
> Likewise, we take these tests each year to keep track of how much you've learned here in school. But like your height and weight, they don't tell us everything, like how much you've learned outside of school or what kind of person you're becoming. These tests might not measure everything, but it's important that you try your best, because they do measure some things.

Like digging up the stories behind the data, I have found that creating analogies to describe the often-complex kinds and uses of data makes them less intimidating and helps us all understand how we can truly use data in positive ways to help our students.

Summary

Data are information that are valuable, useful, and crucial to the success of our students, and to our own success as educators. By incorporating the strategies in this chapter into your daily practice, you may find that your perception of the positive potential of data begins to dramatically shift. I truly hope it does, because as educators, our choice is to either let data be our downfall, or to embrace data and use them to elevate our profession and our students.

Reflection Questions

Now that you have completed the chapter, consider and reflect on the following questions.

1. What are the three most important pieces of data that you use to understand your students? Is there more information that would be useful to you? If so, what are some easy-to-implement tools to obtain it?

2. What is the current culture and climate at your school around openly sharing data? Would you like to encourage more data sharing? What steps could you take to help your school move in that direction?

3. What other analogies have you heard or used to describe data?

4. What digital resources and tools give you access to student and learning data? How can you use these data to benefit students' learning?

IT'S TEST TIME

Think Outside the Bubble on All-Important Standardized Tests

It's that time again. Time to start training your students to fill in the bubbles that too often matter most (whether they are literal bubbles on paper or the computerized versions).

Like it or not, for most teachers, those literal or figurative bubbles determine in large part the public's perceptions of our school and district, our students' opinions of themselves, and our school site's administrators (who may change, for better or worse, once test results come in). Because there is correlation between school ratings and real estate values (Harney, 2013), even real estate agents closely monitor test scores and use them to recommend certain districts and neighborhoods to prospective home buyers. In some places, those test scores also determine whether we are considered highly effective teachers regardless of where and whom we teach.

Perhaps you see standardized test scores as truly indicative of your students' capabilities, and yours. Or perhaps you see them as another reason why high-performing schools will continue to flourish, while other schools continue to languish.

Or, like most great teachers I know, perhaps you see these tests as a necessary nuisance—and although you know they don't tell the whole story, you do see the value in having the students try their best and attain the highest scores they can. If nothing else, you realize that, given the current state of affairs, *not* preparing your students to achieve on these tests could negatively impact their future, your school's future, and even your own. This chapter provides four strategies you can use to help students better perform on standardized tests.

Strategies for Success

Many test-taking strategies are less about being well-prepared for taking tests than they are about teaching students to game the system. For example, many teachers and resources suggest students use the answers a multiple-choice question provides to work backward by plugging those answers into the question and seeing which one works (WilsonPrep, 2017). These sorts of strategies can work to find the correct answers, but they aren't strategies that reflect students' actual learning. Here are four outside-the-bubble strategies to help you focus on this practical picture of standardized test time, and to go further than just having your students use the answers to work backward to prepare for the all-important tests ahead.

Make It About Improvement, Not Perfection

I usually begin my standardized test review about a month before the test begins, and I start by showing my students their results from last year. For my particular students at risk, this usually means a short black line in a bar graph, compared to the much-longer line showing how the rest of the state performed. Instead of having them focus on *their* line, I have them use a highlighter to highlight the area that is open for them to *improve*.

Wherever my students land on that line, to move up one or two levels they often only need to answer *a few* more questions correctly. Some only miss the next level by a question or two. This is a powerful opportunity for us to help foster a growth mindset in our students (Dweck, 2006). Regardless of how students score on standardized tests, it's important that they know and believe that they can improve.

To that end, I then prompt them with the following questions.

1. "Think about how much smarter you are right now than you were last year at this time. Can you answer _____ more questions correctly than you did last year?" Most students will nod confidently and begin to feel motivated at how easily they could move up a level or two.

2. "What can you begin doing right now to make this happen?" I lead the students in making a list that includes everything from getting some more

sleep to looking over tests they have taken throughout the year, reviewing what they previously missed, and spending time to understand *why* they got an incorrect answer.

When your students (and you) realize that you can focus on just a small step of improvement, the tests become less daunting and you can focus on what each student needs to do to advance his or her own learning.

Focus on Celebration, Not Intimidation

I have seen firsthand the positive results of taking a positive, even celebratory, approach to testing with students. As The Rappin' Mathematician, I created a song called "Test Tiiiiime!!!" to help get our school motivated to take a standardized test (Kajitani, 2006). Using the song—which playfully asks, "What time is it?" and answers, "It's test tiiiiiime!"—our school's video club actually made a rap video with students as the stars, and we played it on our closed-circuit television each morning during testing week.

It amazed us all how pumped up the whole school got for testing, and our test results reflected it, as our school more than doubled its growth target that year (California Department of Education, 2008). A teacher from another school told me that although her staff didn't make a video, their principal played the song over the loudspeaker each morning, and even some of the administrators were caught break-dancing in the halls! (Visit www.MathRaps.com to download this song.)

It's also important to celebrate parts of test taking that aren't just the results, so students feel empowered to try their best, and proud of their focus and effort. For example, we can reward the following student behaviors.

- Having perfect attendance during testing days
- Being well-rested and eating a healthy breakfast
- Taking the time to double-check his or her answers
- Providing an answer for *every* question

Rewards don't need to break your budget or be trinkets that you hand out to everyone. They could be privileges like a front-of-the-lunch-line pass for a week, or you could give raffle tickets out and have a drawing at the end of each day with one prize. (Turn it into a lesson on the probability of winning along the way!) Rewarding smart, healthy choices encourages students to continue making those choices well past testing!

Involve the Whole School Community

There are no limits to who should be involved in the testing process. Make sure everyone on your campus knows about and celebrates the testing period. As students purchase their lunch, have the cafeteria staff wish them good luck. Have the maintenance staff talk to students about testing, and have noncore teachers celebrate its importance as well. Our middle school always thanks our elementary feeder schools for their hard work, and the local high school always thanks us.

Of course, it's important to include parents and encourage them to support their students' test taking via meetings, notes, or phone calls home. I believe it can even be beneficial to inform local businesses about testing so that when school-aged kids come into their establishments, they also encourage them. I hold that when students see and hear that their entire community wants them to succeed, it can be a very powerful message that they are part of something greater than themselves and that we're all in this together.

Talk to Your Students About Bias in Testing

If you teach students at risk, this tip is especially relevant to you. Most states' department of education websites make test results available by school, district, income level, and race. They often include research comparisons and commentary on how African American, Latino, and Native American students perform compared to their white and Asian American counterparts, as well as results from poor neighborhoods compared to affluent ones. Sometimes these data can feel discouraging to both teachers and students, but as I wrote about in chapter 6 (page 45), data are about how you use them, and you can use these numbers as both eye-openers and motivators for your students at risk.

If possible, find a school in a poor neighborhood that has stellar test scores (or something equally inspiring and relevant to your students). Then, once you've compiled this information, *share it with your students*. Don't be intimidated to open up the discussion about why you, or your students, believe certain ethnicities score lower or higher on the tests. Keep the conversation respectful but real. Encourage them to rise above the low test scores that have plagued their school, their neighborhood, or their ethnicity. Note that in chapter 9 (page 69), I write about the importance of making ethnic identity an open topic with your students and the care you must take when doing so. You can use those strategies when talking about test data.

In my class, I take this conversation a step further by showing statistics on unemployment by race, high school graduation and college entrance rates, and lifetime earnings. We discuss how and why educators and governments acquire and measure academic performance data and tie these in with how they will help my students be successful throughout their lives. Give your students the opportunity to see the big picture beyond these test bubbles and how they have the power to break from toxic cycles. When you credit their abilities in this way, it motivates them to achieve their best possible future.

Summary

We may never love the emphasis on standardized test scores in our current system, but we can at least make the best of things by taking a positive and strategic approach to preparing students for test success. Here's wishing you, your students, your school, your district, and your community a happy and fruitful testing season.

"What time is it? It's test tiiiiiime!"

Reflection Questions

Now that you have completed the chapter, consider and reflect on the following questions.

1. Think back to your own experiences taking standardized tests. How did you feel? What determined whether you were successful or not?

2. How knowledgeable are your students' parents about standardized tests? What are some ways that you could best communicate helpful test-taking habits and practices with them?

3. What are some creative (or not so creative) ways that you've tried or heard about to motivate students to do well on the tests? Were they effective? How do you know?

4. What is the climate in your classroom on test day and leading up to test day? What could you do to improve it?

PART 2

Owning It With Your Most Challenging Students: Strategies for Succeeding With Students Who are Struggling or At Risk

IT'S ABOUT TIME

Close the Achievement Gap
With Struggling Students

The *achievement gap* is a popular buzzword for students performing below, often far below, their expected grade-level proficiency. However, for these students, the achievement gap is not a buzzword—it is a devastating disadvantage that, if left unaddressed, can severely undermine their opportunity to live successful lives. This affects everyone. A report from McKinsey & Company states this gap "represents hundreds of billions of dollars in unrealized economic gains" in the United States alone (Auguste, Hancock, & Laboissiere, 2009).

I once had an eighth-grade student who I will call Eduardo. Eduardo's classmates constantly poked fun at him for his inability to do simple things, such as add and subtract or tie his shoes. His grades were very low in all his classes, and for as long as he or his mother could remember, he consistently failed in most subjects yet continued to advance to the next grade level year after year.

One day in class, I heard a student tell Eduardo, "You are so dumb, you don't even know how to tell time!"

As he shriveled in his seat, I walked over to Eduardo and quietly asked him if that was true. He confirmed it was. I then asked him the simplest, yet most profound question a teacher can ask: "Why?"

Not allowing him to shrug his shoulders and say, "I don't know," I pressed him for an answer.

Finally, he exclaimed, "Nobody ever taught me!"

"What about your parents?" I asked.

"Nope," he replied.

I then proceeded to take the clock off the wall and explain how it worked. Within ten minutes, Eduardo knew how to tell time. For ten years, nobody had ever taken ten minutes to show him. Many had simply applied a fixed mindset to Eduardo (Dweck, 2006) and dismissed him as unable to learn. He could learn. In fact, he learned quickly and well, and I told him so.

After that day, his confidence began to increase. He became interested in learning, because he knew he could. He began doing his homework and even started performing better on tests.

In this chapter, I take a closer look at how the metaphorical achievement gap affects real students and follow that up with four strategies you can use to help close that gap in your own classroom.

Real Students in the Metaphorical Gap

For many at-risk students like Eduardo, the achievement gap begins well before kindergarten. For some students, it begins at home with parents who are not literate. In addition to struggling to support their children academically, these families often struggle to support them financially, and the concern over whether the family will eat that night far outweighs reading a book to the children before bed. Researchers Betty Hart and Todd Risley (2003) find that a three-year-old raised in a low-income household is typically exposed to *30 million fewer words* than a three-year-old raised in a professional family. For students in this environment, this has a profound effect on their vocabulary growth and ability to interact.

For other students, it begins with parents who do not speak the country's native language. In the United States, that language is English, and we most commonly refer to these students as English learners (ELs) or English language learners (ELLs). The National Education Association (2008) reports "what is most significant—and troubling—is that these students' academic performance is well below that of their peers, and that ELLs have excessively high dropout rates."

As students progress through school, the achievement gap often continues to grow. As teachers, we spend significant amounts of time trying to catch them up instead of focusing solely on the grade-level standards. Students who achieve only half a year's growth for each year they are in school could potentially be six or more grade levels below where they should be by the time they reach the end of their high school career.

Yet, the deep effects of the achievement gap extend far beyond a student graduating high school with the skills necessary to pass an exit exam like the California High School Exit Examination (California Department of Education, n.d.). As a society, we cannot afford to produce eighteen-year-olds who have only a sixth-grade education. We cannot allow to persist an achievement gap that preys on students of color, especially our Latino and African American students. Not addressing this gap means not addressing many of the economic and racial disparities that exist for students in our society.

Fortunately, there are solutions. Although these solutions are deep, varied, and highly debated, the ones we can most effect begin with us, the teachers.

Strategies for Success

Closing the achievement gap with students can involve a variety of strategies, but making your curriculum relevant, retaining good teachers, having targeted training, and connecting with quiet students are all effective strategies you can use *now* in your own classroom, and at your school, to work toward closing the achievement gap for students who are at risk.

Teach Curriculum That Is Culturally Relevant

Let's be honest: a fourteen-year-old student of color living below the poverty line relates much differently to the world than a white student living in an affluent neighborhood. With life experiences so different, why would we even attempt to teach these students the same way? I write on this more deeply in chapter 9 (page 69), but you can start making stronger connections to students by connecting your curriculum content to their own experience.

In one of my classes, when discussing percentages, I pushed aside the standard curriculum to instead discuss dropout, graduation, and unemployment rates among Latino students as well as differences in percentages of students of color attending college. By my making percentages culturally relevant, the students were able to see that percentages are a mathematics concept that applies directly to their lives and their futures. They responded with great eagerness, asking what percentages of Latino citizens are lawyers, teachers, artists, and professional athletes. Once the students saw themselves and their futures in those percentages, I could feel that achievement gap getting just a little bit smaller.

Help Keep Other Good Teachers (Like You!) at Your School

Getting high-quality teachers to come teach in schools with large achievement gaps is tough. Getting them to stay is even tougher. In the United States, the average turnover for all teachers is 17 percent, and in urban schools it's 20 percent (National Center for Educational Statistics, 2015). That means that U.S. schools like mine (and many of yours) are replacing one out of every five teachers each year, which costs the country up to $2.2 billion *every single year* in recruiting, hiring, training, and administrative costs (Amos, 2014).

You can be part of the solution to this turnover problem by fostering school cultures that encourage new teachers to stay at schools with high populations of students who are at risk. Be a team player. Offer to help or support fellow teachers; show your appreciation for what they do. Model commitment to and enthusiasm for teaching students at risk and remind your colleagues publicly what a difference they make and what an important job they have. You will find more strategies for accomplishing this goal in chapter 16 (page 123).

It may sound trite, but it is critical that we keep all teachers motivated and engaged to solve this educational crisis.

Get Targeted Training

To be effective throughout our careers, it's important for teachers to be lifelong learners who continually expand their knowledge base through professional development (Mizell, 2010). To that end, it's important that you advocate for professional development at your school site that addresses sociological as well as practical issues. Become an expert not only on how to overcome teaching challenges but on the larger issues surrounding your students as well—poverty, racism, and gang recruitment.

One of the best staff development meetings we ever had was when the gang-prevention officer from our local police department came and spoke to our staff about his job and its challenges. I learned more from his presentation about the neighborhood in which I teach than in the previous eight years I'd been teaching there.

To schedule something similar, call your local police department and ask what they can set up. Not only is this an opportunity for the teachers and adults on your campus to learn from law enforcement experts, it can also serve as an important way for law enforcement agencies to build bridges between themselves and the communities they serve. When students and the community see police officers on campuses and in classrooms interacting with them and their teachers, true understanding of one another can begin to flourish. Sometimes we can close the achievement gap by building a bridge over it.

Connect With the Quiet Ones

The students slipping through the cracks often aren't the ones all the teachers know; they are the ones whose faces are fuzzy in our brains because their presence in the classroom is barely felt. I once saw one of my middle school students from the previous year, who fit that description, crossing the street in front of my car. She was noticeably pregnant. I couldn't remember her name, and I realized that she had been in my class for an entire year and I had failed to make any significant connection with her during that time. It is in moments like these that I become even more determined to connect with the quiet ones.

Of course, it is a conglomeration of many circumstances that make these students slip outside our grasp, but don't be a contributing factor. Go into your classroom tomorrow, notice each quiet one, and find a way to connect. Some of my favorite ways to connect with quiet students include the following.

- Find nonverbal ways to show them that you notice them, such as a simple high-five or fist bump when you walk by. (You don't need to explain why, just put out your fist so they can bump it).

- If you see an article or video that they might be interested in, bring it in for them. Don't insist that they read or watch it or make a big deal out of it. Just the act of suggesting it to them promotes the connection that you're building.

- Simply say, "Hey, _____" when you walk by them. Quiet students are often used to being walked past without any acknowledgement. A student once told me that when I greeted her by name one morning, it was the first time an adult had acknowledged her since she had left school the day before.

Summary

Closing the achievement gap takes time, commitment, and understanding of the larger cultural and educational issues, as well as the smaller issues that may be happening in an individual student's life, neighborhood, and home. It takes stopping and asking, "Why?" and then working ten minutes at a time, one student at a time, to address a deficit that may have begun long before that student even started school.

In all honesty, I'm not sure what happened with Eduardo. As his life moved on beyond middle school, we did not keep in contact. But at least I know that the next person who asks him for the time will not be disappointed in his answer, and that's a start.

Reflection Questions

Now that you have completed the chapter, consider and reflect on the following questions.

1. What changes could you make in how you teach your curriculum that would make its content more culturally relevant to your students? How might doing so benefit their learning?

2. Is there a teacher at your school whom you know is struggling, or possibly suffering from burnout? What are some things that you could say to that teacher, or some ways that you could encourage him or her?

3. What specific, targeted training do you feel like you need? What other teachers might also like that targeted training, and who could you go talk to about getting it?

4. Name a student in your class whom you don't really know much about. What could you say to him or her *tomorrow* that would help you connect? What could you say the day after that? How would that student's life be different if he or she knew how much you cared?

LET'S TALK ABOUT RACE
Bring Ethnic Identity and Culturally Relevant Curriculum Into Your Classroom

If you teach in a school like mine, where traditionally minority students are actually the majority, yet most of the teachers are white, then it is highly likely that race and ethnicity play a large role in your school culture—even if (*especially* if) these topics are seldom talked about. Consider the following scenarios.

Scenario One: It's 7:30 a.m. on a chilly Tuesday morning, and I'm unlocking the door to my classroom. David (pronounced dah-veed), one of my top students, runs up to me and begins profusely apologizing. "Mr. Kajitani, I'm so sorry. I didn't do my homework last night." Since he is not one to miss his homework assignments, I question him as to why. "My uncle was at work last night, and 'la migra' [what my Mexican American students call U.S. Citizenship and Immigration Services] came to his work and hauled him away. They put him on a bus back to Mexico, and my aunt, who lives with us, was freaking out all night. I couldn't get to my homework."

Scenario Two: At 3 p.m. that same day, at the mathematics department meeting, one of our teachers is distraught because one of her students just accused her of being racist. She explains: "I was describing one of our students, and I said, 'He's a short, black kid

> with glasses.' Another student immediately shouted, 'You're a racist!'
> I don't think using the term *black* makes me a racist, but I didn't know
> what to say."

In the United States, where the race conversation has come to the forefront, we as teachers have the opportunity to create a world in which these critical topics are not something we push aside or work in fear of but rather embrace and make a central part of our daily teaching to everyone's benefit.

We know that ignoring race or being "colorblind" not only doesn't work but actually *harms*—as it refuses to honor a major piece of the identity of every one of us (whether our ancestors come from Latin America, Africa, Europe, Asia, or elsewhere). In *Colormute*, Mica Pollock (2004) writes:

> By using race words carelessly and particularly by *deleting* race words, I am convinced, both policymakers and laypeople in America help reproduce the very racial inequalities that plague us. It is thus crucial that we learn to navigate together the American dilemmas of race talk and colormuteness rather than be at their mercy. (p. 4)

In fact, colorblindness is a position of privilege that many call "the new racism," as it ignores the real experiences of others not in the majority culture (Scruggs, 2009).

In this chapter, I write about how to move past our discomfort and talk about race in our classrooms and schools. More specifically, I write about how you can provide your students, especially your students at risk, with a culturally relevant curriculum—one that considers and incorporates students' specific cultural backgrounds into your lessons to help them thrive academically and personally.

Where to Begin

I get it: race and ethnicity are uncomfortable topics to discuss in our culture. The good news is, there's a whole field of study, within and outside of education, about how to productively understand and address these topics. This is the field I drew on for my master's thesis (Kajitani, 2004), which was about ethnic identity development—and it's the field of study and practice I still draw on when coaching teachers to talk about race.

There's even better news too. As teachers, we have the ear of the next generations in our classroom each day. In learning how to talk about race ourselves, we can also teach students to productively talk about race and ethnicity and provide them with learning via a culturally relevant curriculum. When we can do that, these topics won't be so volatile and uncomfortable in the future, as current students become future cultural leaders.

Strategies for Success

Rather than a series of separate strategies, for this chapter I present a single strategy that comes in three simple steps you can use to begin laying the foundation for opening dialogue and introducing culturally relevant content into your curriculum.

Understand What Ethnicity Is

Although a multitude of academic definitions and debates exist surrounding the term, ethnicity is, at its core, *your affiliation with* your race, country of origin, culture, language, family traditions, and socioeconomics. A culturally relevant curriculum is one that takes the ethnicities of our students into consideration when designing lesson plans.

From using hip-hop to introduce students to literature, to being intentional about showing students examples of successful people who look like they do, to designing project-based learning that addresses specific challenges within the students' community (such as combating homelessness or racism), the key is to find out how our students best learn and what interests them, based on their life experiences, and design lessons accordingly. As distinguished educator and sociologist Pedro Noguera states, "So what I would say that what we really need to do is to encourage teachers to teach the way our students learn, rather than expecting the kids to learn the way we teach" (as cited in Rea, 2015, p. 17).

Understand How Ethnicity Forms

It is only when we begin to truly understand the experiences of our students, their families, and their histories, that we can move toward racial harmony and equality. When we know what has helped shape our students' lives and their perspectives on the world, we can begin to design learning experiences that are truly transformative.

William E. Cross Jr. created a five-stage model for understanding how our students of color go about forming their racial identity. For an enlightening and more in-depth look at his model, I highly recommend reading his book *Shades of Black* (Cross, 1991).

However, to understand our students better, here are the five stages in simple terms (Cross, 1991).

1. **Pre-encounter:** A person who is in the first stage hasn't really thought much about his or her own ethnicity or the ethnicities of others. In fact, he or she is generally happy to go along with what everyone else around him or her believes.

2. **Encounter:** This stage is usually not one that a person chooses to enter on his or her own. Often an event or series of events, such as witnessing racism or being its target, personally impacts and triggers him or her. Once in the encounter stage, a person can no longer fail to acknowledge that different races and ethnicities exist in the world and that a specific community or country treats them differently as a result.

3. **Immersion and emersion:** While immersion refers to the process of *entering*, emersion is the process of *exiting*. In the immersion and emersion stage, a person begins to explore his or her ethnicity and will often surround (immerse) himself or herself with people and symbols of his or her same ethnicity, such as jewelry, clothing, music, and events. All of these convey messages about who he or she identifies with. The person also begins to seek out opportunities to learn about his or her own history and culture and might even begin to develop a great amount of pride in his or her race and ethnicity. At the same time, he or she might also begin to exit (emerge) from other social groups that he or she has previously been a part of or exclude others from that group. It's important to note that it's not always an issue of either immersion or emersion; someone in this stage can be in both at once, or jumping from one group to another. For many people, this stage begins during early adulthood (particularly in college).

4. **Internalization:** Once in this stage, a person begins to gain a sense of security about his or her racial identity. With this security comes a willingness and openness to connect and establish relationships across racial lines.

5. **Internalization and commitment:** In the fifth stage, a person makes a commitment to work toward furthering his or her own understanding of his or her race and ethnicity as well as helping others find their own understandings or meanings.

It's important to note that these stages are not always linear, nor does everyone go through all of them. However, understanding the process that our students go through helps tremendously in our understanding of how we can use ethnicity to provide a culturally relevant curriculum, which I write about in the next section.

Understand How to Use Ethnicity in the Classroom

Consider your understanding of ethnicity and how it forms in your students in the context of what representations of ethnicity actually look like in your classrooms. The term *culturally relevant curriculum* may sound complicated, but it is simply bringing students' cultures into your lessons in creative ways, something we all can do.

Here are three strategies and examples of where to begin:

1. **Tell, ask, and connect:** Tell your story, ask the students for their stories, and then connect what they say to the subject or topic that you're covering in class. In my experience, students, especially students of color, actually love to talk about their ethnicities once you give them the chance. Often, it is we as teachers who are hesitant to talk about it. Begin by simply telling the students about your ethnicity by offering information like the following.

   - Who you are named after

   - Whether your parents or grandparents were born in the nation in which you presently reside; if they weren't, talk about where they came from

   - What your favorite family tradition is

   - What your ethnicity is

   As you talk to students about your background, be ready to own your ethnicity when students ask. My last name is Japanese, and some people find it hard to pronounce. When any of my students, who are mostly Latino, ask me if they can call me "Mr. K." instead of "Mr. Kajitani," I tell them no. I then tell them why—because I'm proud of my ethnicity, which is visible in my name. You can then reflect this back to your students by showing your own respect for their ethnicities. I often continue with a discussion about my students' names and how they can also show pride in their ethnicities.

2. **Turn numbers into people:** Once, as part of a unit on percentages, I asked my students to identify their races, and we calculated what percent of our class was white, black, Latino, and so on. I then pulled up our school's website, and we compared those percentages with our overall school's percentages. We followed that up with percentage comparisons

to our county of San Diego, the state of California, and then the entire United States. No longer were percentages a set of unconnected numbers and mathematics symbols; rather, the students saw *themselves* in those numbers instantly making them real and relevant to their lives.

3. **View arts and literature through a cultural and racial lens:** Alan Sitomer, while teaching English in an inner-city high school in Los Angeles, California, with large numbers of African American students, brings similes to life by having students compare works by classic poets Langston Hughes and William Wordsworth to modern-day rappers such as Tupac Shakur and LL Cool J (Sitomer & Cirelli, 2004). He picks out a line of writing from each and highlights their similarities.

Sitomer—who cowrote the book *Hip-Hop Poetry and the Classics* with Michael Cirelli (Sitomer & Cirelli, 2004), as well as a series of novels geared toward students of color—told me, "By taking popular artists seriously, we can build bridges of access and engagement to core academic concepts. This makes the content relevant and real to our students and expands their worldview in the process" (A. Sitomer, personal communication, May 8, 2012).

Summary

Clearly, these strategies just scratch the surface of the myriad ways we can engage in talking about race and introducing culturally relevant curriculum in our classrooms; however, I hope they spark something for you and provide you with some motivation and ideas to open this dialogue and integrate your students' ethnicities into your classroom lessons.

Once you're motivated, you can find exceptional teaching resources on this topic online, such as the free digital magazine *Teaching Tolerance* (www. tolerance.org), the National Education Association's Diversity Toolkit (www.nea.org/tools/diversity -toolkit.html), and the PBS series *Race: The Power of Illusion* (www.pbs.org/race). There are also dozens of great books on the topic, such as *Why Are All the Black Kids Sitting Together in the Cafeteria* (Tatum, 1997) and *"Multiplication Is for White People"* (Delpit, 2012).

Still, when I present this subject to teachers around the United States, I feel people shifting in their seats with unease; but when I finish, without fail, at least one audience member comes up to me and says emphatically, "*Thank you* for bringing up the topic of ethnicity!" or "That is *exactly* the process I went through myself, but I've never seen it put into words like that!"

On a very deep level, I think we all benefit from talking about race and incorporating it into our classrooms. With a future in the United States and our world that will be more and more ethnically diverse and interconnected, we do a great disservice by ignoring this topic. We have a responsibility to prepare our students as ethnically aware and self-confident, multicultural citizens.

Reflection Questions

Now that you have completed the chapter, consider and reflect on the following questions.

1. What is your ethnicity? How has your ethnicity shaped you and how you see the world?

2. What are the ethnicities of your students? What are some ways that you can incorporate their ethnicities into the lessons you are teaching? What effect do you envision this will have on your students?

3. Why is talking about race so uncomfortable, especially for adults? What would need to change for people to be more comfortable?

4. Think about a story you could tell about your background that would help you connect with your students. What purpose do you want that story to serve, and after you tell the story, what effect do you want it to have on your students?

THE SECRET TO MOTIVATING THE UNMOTIVATED STUDENT

Succeed With Students Who Are At Risk

Let's be honest—as teachers, we often dread a lack of motivation in our students more than any other trait. That dread places our students at risk among the most challenging cases, because they frequently enter our classrooms with a multitude of family and sociological barriers, often paired with well-established track records of low academic achievement. All these things serve to make motivating a discouraged or disinterested student to achieve academically a daunting challenge. That said, it *can* be done.

How do I know it can be done? Because teachers, coaches, and educators are *already* doing exactly this (Lamperes, 1994). How do they do it? This is a complicated issue (of course it is!), but I've come to believe that there is one main factor behind any adult who successfully motivates students who are "unmotivated," at risk, or struggling: *make real connections with them*. Build relationships. Help them feel seen. Believe in them. Have a stake in their success and show it. As Rita Pierson says in her highly regarded TED Talk, "Kids don't learn from people they don't like" (TED, 2013).

We can talk all we want about not having time or how many students we have—and all of this is true—but if you knew that taking a few minutes each week to connect with a struggling, lost student could change the course of his or her life, would you do it? I bet you would. In this chapter, I examine an example of just such a success story and follow that up with three strategies you can use in your own classroom.

A Super Success Story

In 2014, I had the pleasure of talking with Darrell "Coach D." Andrews. Coach D. knows firsthand the plight of students at risk. Raised by a single mother on the public welfare system in Syracuse, New York, Coach D. became a first-generation college graduate, an amazing feat considering he showed up on his college campus unregistered with everything he owned in five garbage bags!

Coach D. went on to become a successful author, motivational coach, and certified speaking professional. When I asked him what critical factors led him down the path to college, rather than dropping out as most of the people he knew had done, here's what he told me (D. Andrews, personal communication, June 1, 2014):

> Instead of looking at factors, I would like to look at people. One of my core philosophies regarding youth and students is simple: A student with a dream is a student with a future; however, a student with a dream is fueled by a caring adult who believes in their dream.
>
> The two people who set the tone for my future were my mother, Constance, and my sixth-grade teacher, Mrs. Palma.

Coach D. went on to tell me how his mother chose to be an example to him when he was in school, returning to school herself and becoming the first in the family to receive a high school diploma—showing her son it was worth doing. And Coach D.'s teacher, Mrs. Palma, "saw beyond the angry boy" he was and told him she would never give up on him. He explained to me (D. Andrews, personal communication, June 1, 2014):

> I was an at-risk youth who had a dream for a better life, and this dream was supported by caring adults.
>
> I have been preaching from the mountaintops for years that we are putting the cart before the horse. Relationships build

successful students. If you put anything else first, you will simply keep going in circles.

I am where I am today because of caring relationships, which then led to textbook excellence.

What a powerful example to show the effectiveness of connecting with and motivating at-risk students!

Strategies for Success

Like Mrs. Palma did for Coach D., teachers must see students not only as they are but *as they can be*. They must see them as *at promise*. Here are three strategies you can use to understand, connect with, and empower your students.

Understand and Honor Cultural Barriers

For years, while speaking sternly or reprimanding my mostly Latino students, I would get increasingly frustrated as I spoke to them, and they would look away, seemingly uninterested in what I was saying. I would demand over and over, "Look at me while I'm talking to you."

A colleague witnessed me doing this and explained that in most of the Latino cultures that our students come from, making eye contact with a superior (the teacher) is actually considered very disrespectful. Oops. Often, fostering a growth mindset (Dweck, 2006) is something teachers need to do within themselves and not just in their students!

From that point on, I began teaching eye contact as a specific skill our students needed to learn, embedding it in weekly lessons. As part of this process, I was careful to respect cultural differences while also helping students learn to distinguish when eye contact is appropriate. I can speak from personal experience that being bicultural or multicultural can be a fantastic advantage in one's life. It's just a matter of learning to navigate the social norms of each.

Just as we can't assume our students walk into our classrooms each day aware of every social norm, we also can't assume the customs we've been raised with are the same as those of our students. Get to know your students' cultural customs and nuances, and when you *ask* students about their culture, you also make deeper connections with them. Remember, the key is to *incorporate*, not eliminate, those differences.

Bring in Success Stories

Sometimes connecting with students who are at risk comes in the form of introducing them to other adults they can connect with—helping them build a team of positive role models to draw from.

Make sure that you and your colleagues are not the only examples of success that your students at risk have ever met. Make the effort to bring in community members who look and speak like your students and who have attained a level of success that they are proud of in fields of study that your students might also pursue. Likewise, ask around for the names of alumni who are successful, and invite them in to speak with your classes. If getting people into your classroom is difficult due to time or distance, take advantage of the technology tools at your disposal by using video conferencing to have them speak to your class directly from anywhere outside the school.

I always tell my students, "*You* define what success is, not the television or a popular YouTuber." (I even have a song about this on one of my Rappin' Mathematician albums.) Once you've booked an outside expert to come in, let the conversation be real and even painful, if necessary. Encourage both the expert and your students to discuss struggles, failures, and successes openly and honestly (within an appropriate framework, of course). Be sure to reinforce this by telling your students that when *they* become successful, you expect that they will come in and speak to the students who then sit at their desks.

Tell Them About Yourself

Sometimes it's hard to get students at risk to open up and talk. Often, it's just not going to happen at all. But just because your students aren't talking doesn't mean they're not listening, perceiving, and thinking. Recall my strategy from chapter 8 (page 61) about connecting with the quiet ones.

Think about a funny story from your life (even better if it happened to you during the age of the students you're teaching). Pull a struggling student aside, and tell him or her the story. Don't expect to get a laugh or reaction; rather, just tell it with pride and confidence. Finish with, "I thought you might like to hear that story," and leave it at that.

The student doesn't have to respond outwardly to the story, but I guarantee you it is something he or she will internalize. Our most challenging students need to know that we are real people, who struggle, who ponder, who overcome, and above all, who care. Get to know your students by giving them, in small bits, a chance to get to know *you*.

Summary

The next time you find yourself intimidated by or frustrated with a student who seems checked out, unmotivated, or unreachable, take a deep breath and remember Coach D.—or some other student of yours who successfully climbed out of the gap. Never lose sight that the key for turning uninterested students into motivated and successful citizens usually begins with a teacher or other adult who simply forms a relationship with them and shows them that they care about them as people—their dreams and their successes in life.

As Theodore Roosevelt famously said, "No one cares how much you know, until they know how much you care" (Goodreads, n.d.c).

Reflection Questions

Now that you have completed the chapter, consider and reflect on the following questions.

1. What are some of the social norms that your students (especially your most challenging ones) struggle with? Why is it important that students understand these norms, and how can you address them so that they can incorporate them into their daily lives?

2. Who are some adults in your school's community that you could bring in, or set up a video conference with, to speak to your students? How do you think your students would respond if you did? Are there ways to make sure your students stay in touch with them?

3. What are some of the ways that you have tried to build relationships in the past? What would you need to do to build lasting, transformative relationships with your students?

4. Why is it important to establish connections with students who are at risk or who might appear to lack motivation?

BEYOND THE BAD KID

Manage Disruptive Classroom Behavior

This chapter was coauthored with Pete Fisher.

A student who is a chronic behavior problem can sink your whole class. All the detentions in the world don't seem to make a difference. Every phone call home seems to end with a nonanswer or a parent who is equally frustrated with the student. It's tempting to peg that student as "the bad kid."

Yet, as teachers, we are still the ones responsible for that student's learning and the learning of his or her entire class. We can't afford to see any student as bad or beyond learning.

As I wrote about in chapter 9 (page 69) and chapter 10 (page 77), when working with students who are struggling or are at risk, we often find ourselves needing to teach much more than the academic content in our books. As many of our students battle poverty, racism, and a widening achievement gap, we're frequently the first ones to see the manifestations of these factors in the ways these students act in class.

Furthermore, these behavioral manifestations often make it difficult, if not nearly impossible, to teach our carefully planned lessons. Dealing with this behavior is critical to our success in teaching struggling students in any classroom while also keeping the rest of the class on track.

If you're determined not to spend the rest of the school year disciplining the same student (or students) with the same results (or lack thereof), it's time to take a deeper look at what is *behind* your students' disruptive behavior and then enact some sensible strategies to effectively handle it.

What Lies Behind the Behavior

It is important to understand *why* a student would act out in class. After all, an individual's behavior always serves a function, even when the person displaying that behavior doesn't understand it. A baby might scream and throw a tantrum for a bottle of food when hungry. An elementary student might hit another child as a form of misplaced affection. A teenager might use profanity to gain peer acceptance and belonging.

All behaviors serve a function for an individual, and the form the behavior takes is actually a process of communication. In each of these examples, the behaviors on display occur because the student did not know any alternative methods to get his or her needs met. As classroom management experts Rick Smith and Grace Dearborn (2016) state, "Students don't act out because they are bad people. They are simply looking for ways to establish and maintain a sense of self while navigating through the sometimes extreme experiences they have" (p. 202). We must also remember that for some time the student has found rewards of one kind or another in his or her behavior. To the student, it might seem that the negative behavior is *working*; he or she is communicating, and someone is paying attention.

As teachers, if we remember this concept, we can start to shift behaviors. We can get to know our students as well as reasonably possible and use our own life experiences, along with some common-sense strategies, to help us figure out what they may be trying to communicate—what they really need—and begin from there.

We all know from experience that there are sometimes obvious explanations for a student acting out, which we may be fortunate enough to learn in parent-counselor-teacher meetings—a breakup of a family, a violent situation, intense peer pressure, the loss of a home, a death in a student's life. In addition, mental-health challenges, especially if undiagnosed, such as ADHD, Asperger's syndrome, or depression, can also help explain disruptive behavior. When we know about these situations, we can work with students to help fill their specific needs, which often changes behavior in class. You don't (and shouldn't) try to fix things alone. Seek the guidance of your school's counselor, psychologist, or nurse. A student's previous teachers can also have great advice, because they have spent many months with that student and could add a much-needed perspective.

Other times, we aren't lucky enough to get a clear picture of what is going on with a student that is causing disruptive or destructive actions. When this is the case, we can still fall back on general tactics to help modify classroom misbehavior even if we do not know its specific roots.

Strategies for Success

Regardless of the cause, there are pitfalls to avoid and steps you can take to ensure the behavior doesn't get out of hand or disrupt learning for other students. Here are five sensible strategies—which build on one another—to deal with negative, unwanted behaviors in your classroom and meet your students' needs.

Maintain Your Self-Control

It's a common saying that the only control we have over another person is that which the person will give us. As teachers, we can try to persuade our students to make effective choices, but we can't physically force them to do so. However, this doesn't mean we have no options to influence their behavior, and it begins with us. Ultimately, we are only responsible for our own actions, and maintaining our own self-control and professionalism ensures the safety and welfare of the students we serve and lets us be appropriate role models.

If something a student says or does infuriates you and makes you feel like screaming or lashing out, instead take a deep breath, and count to five before you respond. Suggesting that both you and the student take the breaths together can be a great way to calm the situation and build a connection. (Hopefully, the next day, you and the student can laugh about how you both had to take some deep breaths!) Research suggests that this simple meditation is effective at reducing symptoms associated with a variety of triggers related to anxiety, insomnia, depression, and attention deficit disorder (Alderman, 2016).

Likewise, you can subtly begin to calm a situation by noticing your posture. Going from standing to sitting, leaning against a wall, or motioning for a student to follow you to a different place in the classroom can give you just enough time (and sanity) to gain control of yourself and, thereby, the situation.

Create an Environment That Fosters Positive Behaviors

When you can maintain your calm, the next step is observing your own classroom and reflecting on whether or not the environment is conducive to students' effective learning and communication. Consider the following factors.

- **Noise:** There are two types of classroom noise: internal (noise you and your students create inside the classroom) and external (noise that happens outside of your classroom but finds its way in and affects the learning environment). External noise, from sirens on a nearby street to loudspeaker announcements, can be quite distracting. Never talk over external noise. Simply pause your voice, wait for it to pass, and then pick up right where you left off. Note that this kind of noise is different from the kind of noise we talked about in chapter 5 (page 37), in which noise reflects students productively engaging with their own learning.

- **Lighting:** Lighting should be bright enough to work but not too harsh. This is something you may have limited control of, but there are steps you can take to mitigate harsh lighting. For example, to soften the light, consider having custodial services remove a few of the fluorescent bulbs in your ceiling, and instead place some lamps around the room. A flickering bulb can cause additional agitation in an already-agitated student, so make sure to get that taken care of as quickly as possible (Dunckley, 2014).

- **Temperature:** It's hard to concentrate when you're cold, and it's hard to focus when you're hot. Making sure your room is a comfortable temperature is important. Again, your facilities can limit your environment, but be cognizant of your options—open a window, bring in a fan, or put in a work order to get your air conditioning fixed.

Remember, factors in the environment often trigger behaviors. If we can limit the number of triggers, chances are we can reduce the potential for negative behaviors.

Offer Clear Alternatives to Negative Behaviors

As teachers in the pressure-cooker culture of many low-performing schools, we often feel we must focus on the academic curriculum without putting much emphasis on building social skills. Yet, many of our students do not have appropriate anger-management, conflict-resolution, or negotiation skills to solve challenges in communication. This stands in the way of learning.

Just like in academics, students need direct teaching, modeling, role playing, practicing, and coaching of behavioral skills. We cannot take for granted, at any age, that students are proficient at these skills. Thus, we must come up with ways to model and communicate to students their alternatives to acting out. For example, when you're feeling stressed or agitated, calmly share these feelings with your students, and then show them how you can pause and take a few deep breaths to calm yourself down.

When there are disagreements between students, use it as a teachable moment, and model some specific phrases they can use to share their opinions in a less-heated way. You may even want to post these phrases on an anchor chart and let students add their own ideas. Consider teaching some basic meditation techniques to the whole class, and perhaps even devoting a few moments each day to quiet meditation. For students who may need the occasional time-out, provide a quiet cooling-off corner.

You must verbally and visually communicate these alternatives in your classrooms and then practice and reinforce them. Unless we offer students real and specific alternatives, they will just continue with behaviors they know already.

Implement Incentives That Align With Needs

Remember, students enact behaviors to get a need met, to protest an activity, or to avoid some type of aversive. Students innately use any behavior that feels on some level like it works for them, which eventually strengthens even negative consequences as a reward. To arrest this behavior, we need to find incentives that are more powerful than what compels them to act out.

This means a lot more than candy bars or class parties. It means asking yourself how you can motivate your students *from within* to behave in new ways. To do this effectively, go back to looking at what they need and aren't getting.

Your incentive will somehow help fill this need. Is it attention they need? How about a class talent contest every Friday after lesson if they behave well all week? Is it stress release? How about organizing a *primal scream* for one full minute before testing day for the school?

The possibilities are endless and demand your creativity, but the point is you can focus on filling students' deeper needs as a true incentive for positive actions.

Work Together, and Have a School Plan

The idea of an entire school being involved in meeting students' needs in ways that encourage positive behavior is a crucial concept for success with students at risk because student behavior problems always manifest beyond just one classroom.

Of course, it's important for each teacher to enact his or her own classroom strategies, but it is *as important* that the larger school community is proactively dealing with behavior issues as well. Thus, all staff members working with students at risk must work together to create a cohesive plan for dealing with escalating behaviors.

The plan needs to include the following.

- **Strategies to prevent escalation:** If possible, train all adults on campus with the same strategies so that there is a consistent language and reaction they can use in times of need. One school I visited even trained parents with the strategies to equip them with positive parenting skills and to create a culture of consistency between school and home.

- **Structured choice:** When students know they have options, they are much less likely to feel forced into something, and a situation can de-escalate. Obviously, offering students a choice in controlling their behavior will look different in a third-grade classroom than it does in a high school history class. You should adjust your approach accordingly.

- **Cooling-off or debriefing areas:** Sending a student to the principal's office usually tells him or her only one thing: you're in trouble. Having designated areas where a student can go and calm down (even if it means screaming and yelling for a while), can be very beneficial and can hopefully be a good place to spend some time without ever making it to the principal's office. It might also be a place that teachers use as well!

- **Consequences and specific conditions for them:** When students make certain choices, we should also make it very clear that those choices often lead to consequences. (The same goes for adults.) Of course, like people, each situation is unique. Having a well-articulated, schoolwide approach can help eliminate confusion and help parents understand why their child was given a certain consequence.

Teams of teachers need to review the plan often and evolve it as the team grows and faces new challenges. Safety should always be the rule but we should always encourage getting creative and trying out new ideas!

If there is not someone on staff already enacting this kind of broader procedure, suggest bringing in a behavior specialist—available through many school-district offices—to work with your team and put a plan in place.

Summary

We've all dealt with the "bad kid" who can disrupt an entire class. But we also know, as teachers of students who are struggling or at risk, that there are often severe and heartbreaking circumstances that may be causing a student to act out.

Whether or not we can find out the specifics of each student's situation, it's our responsibility and our duty to look beyond the behavior at what needs this behavior is communicating and to continually enact strategies to address those needs.

When we do this, we can effectively teach positive ways to communicate and behave and make a tremendous difference in both the life of that student and in the learning of our entire class.

Reflection Questions

Now that you have completed the chapter, consider and reflect on the following questions.

1. Think about a time when you reacted badly during a situation. What emotion were you feeling when you reacted? If you could relive that exact situation, what would you do differently?

2. Think about a time when a student acted aggressively or inappropriately. What do you think he or she was *really* seeking by acting this way? What could you have said, or how could you have fulfilled this need, to calm the situation?

3. Take a moment and look around your classroom. Notice the light, the temperature, and if there are any extra noise or visuals that are competing with what you are trying to teach. Are there steps you can take to improve the environment (maybe a work order for that flickering light, or a poster over the window where distractions occur)?

4. Does your school currently have a campuswide plan to help with student behavior issues? If so, how has your school communicated this plan with teachers, students, and parents, and are there places where it can improve this communication? If not, what barriers must it remove to start putting one together?

NO, OR QUID PRO QUO?

Negotiate With Students Who Are Struggling

Think about the best negotiator you know. Is it a businessperson who can close any deal? It is a lawyer who knows how to convince a skeptical jury? Or, perhaps it's a child who always seems to end up with the front seat in the car or the last cookie in the jar? Whoever it is, I'll bet he or she enjoys the art of negotiation that moves people forward.

As teachers of students who are struggling or are at risk, it is crucial that we also embrace this art of negotiating and moving people forward. It's a matter of survival. We also know that in a full classroom of high-need students, negotiations can become unclear, confusing, and sometimes downright messy—and getting mired in them can stall the learning at stake for everyone.

Negotiating with a student starts with us and being conscious of our posture. In my experience, crossing your arms and hovering above a student with a scowl on your face is a sure way to build an immediate wall between you and your student. Instead, assume a relaxed posture or sit down next to the student, shoulder to shoulder. Sitting next to a student in this way sets a tone of you both looking in the same direction as opposed to sitting across from the student, which can create more of a standoff situation.

Where chapter 11 covered strategies for addressing particularly disruptive students, this chapter focuses on understanding how to negotiate efficiently and effectively in your classroom with *all* your students. This is critical to maintaining the flow of your lessons and ensuring that your class runs smoothly. It allows you to get to teaching the content *they* need to understand for success in school and life. In this chapter, I present some ways you can find common ground with your students and follow that with four strategies you can use in your own classroom to achieve that ground.

Negotiation Starts With Common Ground

Understanding a student's motivations is essential to successful conflict resolution and choosing a negotiation strategy. The stalls we face with messy negotiations usually come down to one problem: *misaligned objectives*. For example, although a teacher's objective may be to have students calculate the Pythagorean theorem, identify an alliteration, or name all of the parts of an atom, a struggling student's objective for the class could be something quite different. It may range from an attention-seeking desire to disrupt class to simply staying awake.

Try as we might, we probably can't convince our students to see that we all should have the same objective in school—learning. But we need not let misaligned objectives stop us from helping learning happen.

To overcome opposing objectives, you need to use every successful negotiator's first important strategy for success: *finding common ground*. To do this, shift your focus from the student's objective (say, to disrupt the class) to his or her need (perhaps, some attention). Observe a student who is off task and ask yourself, "What does he or she need?" As I wrote in chapter 11 (page 83), perhaps it is just some acknowledgment, a safe space, or a way to let off some steam.

Often, these needs are easy to meet—offer an encouraging comment or a one-minute foot-stomping break. Once you have shown your student that you understand his or her need, you have placed yourself on common ground and in the optimal position for successfully negotiating with him or her to return to the lesson at hand.

Strategies for Success

Once you've established common ground, you can use any number of approaches to move your students back to task. Here are four concepts and examples to keep in mind as you practice fine-tuning your classroom negotiation skills.

Use Reciprocity to Build Relationships

One of the most obvious negotiation strategies, reciprocity, relies on the principle of "Do this for me, and I'll do this for you." Although it is often the simplest and quickest way to resolve a conflict, it can also result in creating a climate of expectations in which a struggling student will only work when given something in return.

Counteract this by using reciprocity in the context of building on the student-teacher relationship and building on the student's ultimate goals. Start with reciprocity that is small and immediate but grows into something that is long-term and more gratifying for the student. For example, I had a student I'll call Luis who always fell asleep in class. One day, we struck a deal that if he could just stay awake for an entire class period, he would earn a front-of-the-lunch-line pass.

After two days, we agreed that since this was becoming easy for Luis—and he was getting something positive out of being present in class—he now needed to stay awake for three consecutive days in order to earn the pass. However, since he was now accomplishing more, I offered more as well: at the end of the new three-day goal, he got to bring a buddy to the front of the lunch line. (This gave his buddy even more incentive to make sure Luis stayed awake in class!)

In all honesty, Luis still fell asleep on occasion; however, it was no longer a daily event, and whenever this happened, we started his three-day cycle over. By then, we had built on the relationship enough so that, when I enacted our agreement, he accepted it easily.

It's also important in situations like this one to consider how some student behaviors can reflect an environmental or underlying health condition. For example, a constantly sleepy student may have conditions at home that inhibit proper sleep habits, and there are multiple sleep disorders that cause chronic fatigue. These conditions aren't under your control, so when you can use a strategy like reciprocity to productively motivate students to work past them, it's to everyone's advantage.

Establish Consistency

Students are often off task not because they don't want to be participating in the class activity, but because they are unclear as to what you expect of them. Many of our students at risk lack consistency in their personal lives and at home. Many have parents who are constantly working, forcing students to fend for themselves when it comes to food, homework, and bedtime. Often, school is the only place that is a constant in their lives.

Thus, it is crucial that your classroom routines, procedures, and expectations are *consistent*. Consider the following ideas.

- **Post the daily schedule (in the same place) every day:** No student should ever have to wonder, "What are we doing today?" or "What are we doing next?"

- **Make sure to clearly post your expectations:** When a student is not fulfilling an expectation, you can easily point it out (or, ask the student to tell *you* which expectation he or she is not following). It is important that students see you consistently and fairly reinforcing the expectations you post.

- **Make it contractual:** Start the year by having the students and their parents sign a contract about what you expect of them and what they can expect from *you* throughout the school year. Don't let it be just another piece of paper that all parties sign and forget about; instead, be sure to consistently refer to the contract (at least once every two weeks).

These strategies not only help your students learn but help you avoid the constant and unsuccessful messiness of negotiating with students about what they should be doing at any given time.

If you use consistency when one of your students is off task, you need remind him or her only of the *procedure* that he or she is not following; you do not need to get into a discussion about the behavior. This will save you much-needed time and energy (not to mention your voice) throughout the day.

If you haven't read *The First Days of School, Fourth Edition* by Harry K. Wong and Rosemary T. Wong (2009), run out and get it immediately. It is a seminal book on classroom procedures and a fantastic guide to designing, implementing, and enforcing consistency in your classroom. As they state, "A well-managed classroom has a set of procedures and routines that structure the classroom. The procedures and routines organize the classroom so that the myriad of activities that take place there function smoothly and are stress free" (Wong & Wong, 2009, p. 84).

Use the Value of Social Validation

I remember growing up as a child, and the McDonald's near my house displayed the famous sign: "Over 1 million served." As we all know, that sign soon came to say, "Over 1 *billion* served." Each time I see that sign, I have an uncanny urge to go back to my meat-eating days, drive over, and order a Big Mac. Why? Because if so many others are enjoying themselves at McDonald's, then I should too, right?!

Likewise, how about the commercials for the latest pharmaceutical drug, which state, "Ask your doctor about *thing x*, and join millions of others who have found relief . . ."? Whether we like it or not, there is something to this classic bandwagon advertising principle, which allows us to feel connected to others and part of a larger group. As teachers, we can make productive use of this principle to guide the actions and outcomes of our students in a positive direction.

Sometimes, a new student comes into my class in the middle of the year, often because he or she was kicked out of his or her previous school. Immediately upon guiding the new student to his or her assigned seat, I publicly welcome him or her into my classroom, and after introducing the new student, I ask the class to give the *two-clap welcome*. (This is two claps in unison, followed by everyone shouting, "Welcome!" together.) I then assertively say, "This is a great class, and you will enjoy being here. Everyone knows *exactly* what he or she needs to be doing at all times!" Not only does this reinforce the consistent routines in my class but also sends a clear message that if you want social validation in my class, you'd better be doing what everyone else is.

Sometimes, when a student is off task, I'll simply walk over to him or her and quietly whisper, "Look around at your classmates. Every single one of them is working except for you. I need you to be productive like everyone else." This kind of statement can work well with an otherwise-engaged student who is simply off task, but remember each situation and student is unique. This is probably not the best approach when confronting a student who is *seeking* to disrupt class. (Refer to the strategies in chapter 4, page 29, and chapter 10, page 77).

Motivate Through Scarcity

When you're at the store, and you see that there's only one bag of cookies left, do you grab it a bit more quickly than you normally would? Of course you do. If you don't, someone else might grab it, and you'll be left without your precious Oreos! When you order something from the internet, the first thing you want to know is "How quickly can I get it?" Although you've lived your entire life without it, suddenly you need it now. Scarcity of resources and scarcity of time get us to act quickly. Utilize this knowledge in your classroom.

When practicing a mathematics problem, I'll sometimes say, "You have exactly two minutes and thirty seconds to complete this problem." Rarely will students ever stop to ask, "Or what?" They're too busy working. If they do, I simply reply, "Now you've only got two minutes and ten seconds."

At the end of class, to gain closure on the lesson, I often utilize exit tickets, where the students have to complete a problem on a small scrap of paper in order to leave the classroom. If they don't act quickly, they don't get to leave the classroom on time. To avoid making this feel punitive, the key is to select problems or tasks that the students can actually complete in the time you've allotted. You don't actually want them to be late for their next class, but it can happen from time to time.

Once, after holding a student an extra minute after lunch began, he said sadly, "Now all the good food will be gone. I'll have to eat the chicken nuggets." *Exactly*, I thought to myself. (And, ugh, can we please talk about school lunches?) Exit tickets work great for any subject and level and are a great way to formatively assess learning.

From scarcity of time to scarcity of cafeteria food, use this negotiation tactic to keep your students moving.

Summary

Negotiating with a struggling student can be a daunting task. Negotiating with a room full of them can be downright intimidating. However, if you view these negotiations with creativity and fairness, and if you use the four tactics in this chapter to effect a positive outcome, you will find that you can turn even the most unwilling student into one that is on board and on task. In so doing, your classroom becomes one that consistently moves forward in the direction of learning.

Reflection Questions

Now that you have completed the chapter, consider and reflect on the following questions.

1. What expectations for behavior and performance do you have for your students? How have you communicated these expectations with them? Are they stated clearly and posted in your classroom?

2. Imagine a student walking into your classroom and immediately saying, "What are we doing today?" Now imagine a student walking into your room, already knowing "what we're doing today," without having to ask. What would you need to do to make that shift?

3. What specific procedures and routines are happening in your classroom that the students have shown that they are able to do very well? What can you say, do, or display to communicate this success in order to keep everyone doing it regularly?

4. How could you combine scarcity of time with using exit tickets to wrap up the end of class and keep students focused until the very last moment?

THE UNINVOLVED PARENT

Reel Parents in With Three Basic Strategies

When calling the parents (or guardians) of students at risk, most teachers in low-performing schools have had the exact same experience, many times over. It goes something like this:

> Ring, ring . . .
>
> Ring, ring . . .
>
> Ring, ring . . .
>
> Ring, ring . . .
>
> *(Hang up phone.)*

If we are lucky enough to catch a parent, it's not uncommon to find a less-than-enthusiastic person on the other end of the line, a person who seems uninterested in improving his or her child's behavior or academic performance.

Convincing some parents to come onto our campus to meet with teachers is harder than the gum under our students' desks. However, we can't give up. I do believe it is a part of our job as teachers to help bridge the gaps in their families as well as their classrooms. Getting parents or guardians invested in their children's education is a critical factor in reaching students who are struggling or at risk and in helping them succeed.

Connect with an uninvolved parent, and you can potentially turn your most challenging student into a valuable part of your classroom culture. To that end, in this chapter, I examine some strategies you can use to establish that connection.

Strategies for Success

Three of my favorite strategies for hooking uninvolved parents are utilizing technology to improve communication, offering free food and childcare (bear with me), and thinking like a salesperson. Each of these is a creative and effective strategy you can use to get parents involved in improving students' learning.

Utilize Technology to Communicate

Technology can be very useful when trying to communicate. For example, I remember leaving a voicemail message for a friend and found myself feeling a little offended when, five days later, he hadn't returned my call but had been very active on his Facebook page. However, instead of dwelling on the fact that he was able to spend so much time chatting online but not call me back, I simply left him a short message on his Facebook page. He responded to me immediately.

We live in a fast-paced, up-to-the-minute, technology-driven world, where communication happens online, in real time, and consists of two or fewer sentences. Not only that, but many people have a strong preference for written, digital communications rather than a traditional phone call and will respond to a quick text-based message much more quickly. Why not apply these principles to getting parents involved?

Get a parent's cell phone number and offer to send an update of his or her child's performance via text. (I've found that the best time to get a parent's cell phone number is at the beginning of the school year when everyone is off to a fresh start.) It could be as simple as "Miguel was off task today. Please speak with him when you see him" or "Valerie just got an *A* on her mathematics quiz." Or better yet, take a photo of Valerie holding up her test with the big *A* written on it, and text it to the parent. Consider sending the text while the student is right in front of you so that your relationship with the parent is visible to the student. It conveys to students that everyone has their best interest at heart.

Perhaps this will not get parents into the school for a meeting, but it will certainly keep them more involved. When you do get a parent to agree to come onto campus, be sure to send him or her a text an hour or so before the meeting as a reminder.

There are other steps you can also take to engage parents through technology. For example, you could start a class Facebook page, blog, or teacher website to give parents the option to drop in virtually, whenever they please. Most simple sites or pages take mere minutes to set up, and parents will be able to sign up, sign in, and get involved as often as they want.

Remember that each time parents leave a comment, like the page, or check what homework you have assigned, they are choosing to engage. Be sure to thank them for staying involved!

Offer Free Food and Childcare

Let's be honest here: which would you rather go to, a free meeting or a free meal?

When inviting a parent in to discuss a student's issues, mention that you'll have coffee and muffins, popcorn and fruit, or whatever—and let him or her know that you'll have enough for any siblings present as well.

If you're lucky, the parent might even show up with some food to share. Working in a predominantly Latino neighborhood, where sharing food is a cultural norm, I've enjoyed eating more than a few delicious *pupusas* as the result of a parent meeting. Like I wrote in chapter 9 (page 69), never underestimate the value of understanding the culture your students and their families come from.

If a parent does bring the student's siblings, there is additional preparation you can undertake. We all know how frustrating it can be to try to conduct a parent meeting while younger siblings are running around (or out of) the classroom. Plus, I often feel bad when having an honest conversation with a parent and student, and a younger brother or sister (who usually looks up to his or her older sibling) is sitting there listening to less-than-stellar things being said about the student.

Consider teaming up with another teacher not involved in the meeting (or who might also want to meet with that parent after you), and set him or her up in that teacher's room or a corner of your room with some age-appropriate books, supervised games, or activities that the younger siblings can participate in while the conference is taking place. It might require you to repay that teacher with twenty minutes of your time later; however, we all know that getting a struggling student back on track pays for itself in the classroom management department!

Think Like a Salesperson

A good friend of mine is a toy salesman. Part of his job includes cold-calling toy stores to make appointments with store managers to come by and show them the latest products. The problem? For a time, he found it very difficult to get in touch with any of them.

So, he changed his approach. After leaving a message with his name and number, he began saying, "Tell _____ I'll call back at 3:30 this afternoon." Sure enough, when he called back at the specified time, he suddenly found that many managers were expecting his call.

When leaving a message for a parent, try simply telling him or her that you'll call back at 7:30 p.m. that night. (Be sure to call at that time!) Not only does it take the pressure off the parent to call back but gives the parent room to set up open time to take the call (rather than feel interrupted in the middle of dinner) and unofficially makes both you and the parent accountable for the communication.

Then, when you begin the conversation, start with something *nice*. My toy sales-man friend begins conversations with commenting on how happy everyone in the store seems, or how clean the floors are, because he finds that it makes the store managers much more likely to feel comfortable and relaxed. Don't our students' parents deserve the same?

Many parents of struggling students have been experiencing phone calls from teachers for years, telling them how badly behaved their children are, or how they never do their homework. Consider starting the conversation by complimenting something the student has done recently (even if you have to dig deep into yourself to find something). If you've reached the point of calling home, it's likely you've already used some of the strategies I presented in chapters 10–12. If you have, that should offer you plenty of connection points to highlight that student's most positive attributes or contributions and establish with the parent that you deeply value his or her child as a person, despite any problems or challenges you must relate. This will not only help establish rapport with the parent, but it might just encourage him or her to pick up the phone the next time you call!

As much as I hate what I'm about to say, I'm just going to say it anyway: some-times, you just won't be able to get ahold of a parent. They won't call back, they won't show up, and when you ask the student about it, all you will get is a blank stare and a shrug of the shoulders. When this happens, know that you've done the best that you can, and never hold it against the student. Keep moving forward, keep believing in the student, and keep letting him or her know that you value him or her.

Summary

Each day, parents send their children into our schools and classrooms, trusting us to teach them, to feed them, and to help them pursue their dreams. There are times when hooking an uninvolved parent can be frustrating. I once heard a colleague liken it to "trying to chase a mouse around the house with a spoon." However, with creativity, technology, and some free cheese, we might soon find ourselves face-to-face with that parent, discussing plans to help his or her child be successful and pursue his or her dreams.

Reflection Questions

Now that you have completed the chapter, consider and reflect on the following questions.

1. What ways are you currently using technology to communicate directly with parents or keep them informed of what is happening in your classroom and at your school? Are there any barriers that stand in the way of being able to communicate with parents more frequently (such as language barriers)? How can you overcome these barriers?

2. Is there another teacher on your campus that you would consider teaming up with, in order to have him or her supervise younger siblings, while you conduct a parent meeting? What kind of arrangement or agreement could you suggest so that it's a win-win-win for you, that teacher, and the parent?

3. Based on your experiences, how have parents reacted when you have called them to discuss students? How have you successfully turned a difficult start into a successful resolution?

4. Think about how you want parents to feel when you call them at home. What are some specific things you can say to make them feel this way?

STUDENT-LED CONFERENCES
Empower Students by Putting Them in Charge

This chapter was coauthored with Mindy Crum.

When you, as a teacher, encourage students to take ownership of their learning and their results, more often than not, you will find they take that responsibility seriously. When I (Alex) was a student, I loved going to my parent-teacher conferences. I remember sitting around my teacher's desk with my mom and teacher early in the morning before the school day began, eagerly awaiting the grown-up conversation.

Of course, I attended school in a middle-class neighborhood in a high-achieving district, and my mom was very involved in my education. As I consistently earned good grades, I often left the conferences beaming with pride at all the nice things my teachers said about me. Unfortunately, this is not the reality for many students, especially students who are struggling or are at risk.

For these students, parent-teacher conferences are a half hour (or more) of teachers telling their parents or guardians how many homework assignments they haven't completed, how poor their scores were on the latest round of standardized tests, and how they need to modify and improve their behavior. That is, assuming the parents even show up at all. (Make sure to review the strategies in chapter 13 [page 99], for keeping parents engaged.)

This format and experience—of teachers talking at parents while the student sits idly by—only further discourage already-challenged students and rarely lead to improvement. In this chapter, we introduce a different kind of conference, one that puts the students in charge of briefing their parents, and follow that up with detailed strategies for making this format effective.

A New Kind of Conference

What would you say if I told you there is a way to make teacher conferences an opportunity for struggling students to engage and walk away feeling empowered rather than dejected? Enter, the *student-led conference*. This conference format allows all students to take an active role in their own learning and development and still gives parents an opportunity to gain the teacher's perspective.

Not only does this format give students a leadership role (something often lacking in traditional schooling of at-risk students), it also gives them the ability to prepare data, present information, and answer questions—all real-life skills that are critical to academic and career success.

I've found student-led conferences to be a revelation for my students who are at risk, as has Mindy Crum, an experienced teacher of this student population, whom I asked to coauthor this chapter. After implementing student-led conferences at our low-performing schools, we both experienced a positive shift in students' attitudes before, during, and after parent conferences.

In a study about student-led conferences, Sharon Jackson (2012) finds that students enjoy not only leading the conferences but also the process of goal setting and sharing the information with their parents. In addition, parents like when their children can use life skills such as responsibility, reflection, and leadership.

Strategies for Success

Rather than present multiple, separate strategies, here, we present seven steps you can take to have your students run their own conferences *this* year, and give them an opportunity to think critically, speak articulately, and own their learning. Each section represents the next step in the process.

Select and Announce Dates

When trying this format for the first time, selecting conference dates and announcing them to students and their parents at the beginning of the school year secures your commitment to running your conferences differently from past years. It also gives the students time to process that they really will be conducting their own conferences and gives them a timeline of how much they'll need to prepare. Note that this is important, even if you've already used this format for several years.

Some of the most effective ways to let students and parents know about conferences is by sending home a note at the beginning of the school year, making the announcement at back-to-school night, or communicating it on social media. Also, be sure to talk about the benefits of student-led conferences. I suggest taking photos the first time you try it so that you can share photos the following years, giving students and parents a sense of how much fun it is!

Perhaps your school site or district already has prearranged days for parent conferences, often only once per school year. If so, we suggest adding a second conference period during the school year and even a third, year-end conference period to give students and parents maximum benefit from this format.

Although this does take some extra planning and practice, once the structure is in place, we have found that conferences (and the time between conferences) become a pleasure, as the students engage and improve more each time. You can use the third conference to close out the school year to celebrate reaching goals, honor working through challenges, or simply reflect on learning that has taken place.

Mindy also found that she can save time by scheduling more than one parent conference concurrently. Since students do most of the talking, she can bounce around the room and sit in on conferences that are occurring simultaneously. See Hold the Conference for more details (page 111).

Engage in Ongoing Communication

Communicating with parents is essential for successful student-led conferences. Even though parents have known about the conferences since you first announced them at the beginning of the school year, be sure to notify them again several weeks prior to the conference week. Use the strategies in chapter 13 (page 99) to make sure they know that it is critical that they attend.

Make it clear to parents that *their child* will be running the conference and what an exciting opportunity this is to see their child in action. This often takes the pressure off of parents, especially those who are English learners, and makes them more likely to come.

Make sure to offer a wide range of conference times to ensure that parents can attend at their scheduled time. Place the responsibility on the students for getting their parent (or parents) there and teach them reminder tools such as writing it on the calendar at home, leaving written reminders on the refrigerator (or other high-traffic areas), or sending reminder texts or emails to reinforce the importance of attendance. When sending communication home, be sure you send it in the parents' native language. You can always have your students help translate the letters.

Gather Data

Just as an effective sales presentation would include relevant data, any student conference should as well. Give students a clear picture of what information they will be responsible for sharing during their conference (attendance, grades, work samples, standardized test scores, and so on). Help them understand the information they will be presenting, why it is important, and how to effectively showcase it. Remember, data should not be something that you collect, pull out for conferences, and then tuck away again. Rather, data collection should happen at the beginning of the year, and throughout the school year, so that students are very familiar with it come conference time (it also prevents a last-minute rush to gather the things they need).

Prior to the actual conference, have students spend time analyzing the data, perhaps comparing them with other students (a built-in mathematics lesson!), and organizing them. This organization should also include other information students will present, such as goal binders, reading levels, and recent test or homework scores, as well as a big-picture idea of how all aspects fit together.

Complete a Checklist

After students have gathered and organized their data, they should complete a checklist. An easy way to provide this is to create a shared online document (like a Google Doc), so students can access it from anywhere, and you can peek in on their progress from time to time. This checklist ensures that the students are well prepared and thorough, but it can also serve as a guide for them to use *during* the conference. Mindy includes a list of items the students are to share with their parents (such as homework and reading logs), test scores, semester goals, and the student's leadership role in the class. She also includes a spot at the end to determine new goals at the end of the conference.

You can create your checklist any way that works for the data your students will share with their parents. Make sure not to leave anything to the last minute—have students complete the checklist at least a week prior to the conference as well as get their materials ready (data notebooks, test scores, writing samples, and so on). This helps them feel relaxed and invested in getting their parents to the conference to see the work they have prepared.

Of course, not all information that students share will be glowing reviews, and it can be very intimidating for students when they know they will be sharing information that their parents won't like. However, I've found that when a student has to own it himself or herself, it allows for a conversation between him or her, his or her parents, and the teacher that is authentic and real and can help put the student on the path to success.

Conduct a Dress Rehearsal

Like any good presenter, students need time to practice, and for many, running a meeting will be a new experience. Of course, the more public speaking practice you can give them prior to the conferences, the better. Focus on fundamental speaking skills such as speaking in a loud, clear voice; maintaining eye contact; and assuming appropriate posture, which are critical skills that will serve them well during the conferences and throughout their lives. You can have students practice public speaking to each other and even have a rubric that the listeners fill out (see figure 14.1).

Conference Leader's Name: _____

Did the Conference Leader:	Yes	Somewhat	No
Speak loudly	❑	❑	❑
Speak clearly	❑	❑	❑
Use eye contact and proper posture	❑	❑	❑
Share important information	❑	❑	❑
Thank everyone for coming	❑	❑	❑
Additional comments:			

Figure 14.1: Rubric for students practicing their public-speaking skills.

*Visit **go.SolutionTree.com/instruction** for a free reproducible version of this figure.*

When it comes to practicing for these conferences, it is most effective (and fun) when done with another adult acting as the parent. Recruit your principal, media specialist, nurse, on-campus adult volunteers, and other teachers who are considering incorporating student-led conferences into their own practice. If necessary, first model for students how to share their data while using the checklist as a guide. Explain to the stand-in adults that their role is to be a listening guide and to ask clarifying questions as necessary.

It is important that you make the practice authentic to the situation students will face at the real conference. Set up stations in the room where the conferences will be held. If students will be speaking primarily in a language other than English, have them practice in that language as well. A student whose parents speak only Spanish should not have to translate his or her words for the first time in front of his or her parents. If the actual conference is scheduled for fifteen minutes, have students practice for the equivalent amount of time.

If you are not able to recruit adults, you can always pair up students, taking turns in the roles of student and parent, or ask students from higher grades to fill in.

Finally, if you will need a translator for any of your conferences, make sure to find and schedule him or her in advance. If your school does not automatically provide a translator, reach out to a parent liaison, a staff member who lives in the community, or the students themselves to find someone who can help. I've even had younger and older siblings step in at the last minute.

Consider Your Room Configuration

A room's configuration is extremely important, especially if you have several conferences occurring at once. As many parents (especially those who do not speak English well, or who come from a different culture) are often intimidated or uncomfortable in a school, be sure to create a warm and welcoming environment.

Playing quiet classical music is very helpful in both creating a relaxed atmosphere and preventing separate conference groups from overhearing each other if you are having students conduct concurrent conferences. Have the student data and checklists easily accessible at the entrance of the classroom, such as in a folder in a file box or on a digital tablet (like an iPad) placed on a desk at the entrance.

When setting up conference stations, we recommend positioning two desks next to each other with four chairs (one each for the student, parent, teacher, and interpreter, if needed). I recommend having an extra chair handy should the student have more than one parent present. Set up the conference stations in the corners of the room, which creates maximum spacing between groups for privacy. It is also a good idea to have the student and parent sit next to each other (not across from each other), so that both can see and read what the student presents.

Hold the Conference

As you talk up the conferences in the week prior, students will become both anxious and excited. Take this opportunity to explain that these are normal emotions, but keep students focused on the goal of running a productive conference that will result in the development of their speaking and leadership skills. Trust that they will become empowered through the process of sharing, discussing, and understanding their own learning by articulating it to their parents. Although you will need to schedule your conferences based on your needs and the time your school schedule allots, we've found that twenty minutes is the ideal length of time. This offers plenty of time for the student to speak (about ten minutes), the teacher to add perspective (five minutes), and the parent to ask questions (five minutes).

As the conferences get underway, float from one conference to another (if you have chosen to schedule more than one at the same time), making sure to double-check that students are correctly using the checklist. Of course, anticipate that some students will need you to be physically seated there for the entire conference, and schedule and plan accordingly.

Finally, find a way to close the conference in a way that is positive and action-driven. For example, consider ending the conference with the student, parent, and yourself signing the conference checklist where you allotted space for new goals. Be sure to copy the checklist and send it home as soon after the conference as possible. If time allows, it can also be fun to take a photo of the student at the conference with his or her parents (hopefully with everyone smiling). You can use this photo to email the parents later and thank them for coming, and to show next year's students.

Summary

We found teachers who have not conducted a student-led conference before often wonder if they are worth all this effort. Our answer, unequivocally, is *yes*! We find that students', parents', and our own experience of conference time transforms for the better when we implement student-led conferences. Although it requires more effort and organization up front, we find conference time to be both easier and much more rewarding this way.

By taking responsibility for clearly communicating their own progress and goal setting, students improve not only their learning engagement and confidence but their oral language skills as well. We've also watched with joy as parents listen intently to their child's sharing of successes and struggles, which can serve to strengthen the lines of communication between them.

Great conferences needn't be a rarity, even for struggling students. When you hold student-led conferences at regular intervals, it offers these students an opportunity to not just survive in the academic world, but to take an empowering leadership role in it.

Reflection Questions

Now that you have completed the chapter, consider and reflect on the following questions.

1. What has been your experience with parent conferences, especially with the parents of your students who are struggling or are at risk?

2. In what ways are you getting students and their parents excited about attending parent conferences and making sure they come at their scheduled time?

3. What specific data do you normally discuss at parent conferences? What effect would it have on the student if he or she were the one presenting the data, and what would you need to do in advance to familiarize him or her with this information?

4. After reviewing the list of seven steps outlined in this chapter, what challenges do you anticipate? What might be a way to proactively address these challenges with your students?

PART 3

Owning It at Your School and District: Strategies for Succeeding as a Member of a Staff Team

MAKING MEETINGS AN HOUR TO EMPOWER

Turn "Not Another Meeting!" Into "Let's Get to Business!"

As teachers, we have a lot on our plates. As a result, we have a lot to discuss—and that discussion usually takes place in the form of a meeting. The problem? There's at least one meeting every day!

From individualized education plans to behavior support plans, my own grade-level team seems to hold more meetings than there are topics to discuss. Likewise, when it comes to meetings about our students, especially students in crisis, there is a lot at stake in each discussion.

Although we don't have time to waste in long and unproductive meetings, that doesn't mean that meetings aren't crucial for keeping schools and teaching teams functioning. They are! Critical issues, such as determining what is essential to learn in each content area, developing common assessments, and learning new strategies from each other, are only a few of the things we need to discuss. Thus, effective communication and collaboration are imperative for helping our students.

In this chapter, I write about the cultural importance of meetings between teachers and follow that up with four strategies you can use to make the most of your meeting time.

The Cultural Importance of Meetings

In an interview with Fast Company (www.fastcompany.com), consulting expert William R. Daniels states, "Meetings matter because that's where an organization's culture perpetuates itself. . . . So if every day we go to boring meetings full of boring people, then we can't help but thinking this is a boring company" (Matson, 1996). Although Daniels's work focuses on the culture of companies, his findings apply equally to schools.

Devalue a meeting, and we simultaneously devalue a chance to make a collective difference in the lives of those who need us most—our students. Although running a meeting might not be in our initial job description as a teacher, it's one of those things we often end up doing. In most of the meetings I've been in, the principal isn't in the room to facilitate, so it's up to us, as teachers, to make sure we productively use the time. When teachers, and everyone else involved in the meeting, know how to make that meeting productive, the students win.

Strategies for Success

When considering how to make your meetings efficient and productive, there are of course the standby rules of starting on time, keeping discussions on topic, and so on. Beyond that, though, it is imperative that every teacher and staff member leave each meeting feeling focused and empowered. Here are four strategies to accomplish a deeper level of empowerment and productivity in your meetings.

Ask (and Answer) These Two Questions

I find every successful meeting includes two critical questions that each participant must know how to answer: Why are we here today? and What is the plan? The former is a question to ask at the meeting's inception, while the latter is something to answer at its conclusion. Let's start with the former.

Just as a highly effective teacher rarely must answer the question, What are we doing today? (because students have been trained to find the daily objective and agenda), a highly productive meeting never includes participants who sit there wondering, "Why are we here?" Thus, address this head-on by answering it immediately at the beginning of each meeting.

You can simply have a team member ask the question aloud (in a positive, warm tone) with the person leading the meeting answering it, or the person running the meeting can start with, "The purpose of this meeting is . . ." When the meeting leader has a well-thought-out finish to this opening question, it helps him or her, along with the group, stay focused during the entire meeting.

Likewise, each participant must be aware of the goal he or she is moving toward—having a plan. Just as a well-planned lesson never leaves students wondering, "What should I do next?" a productive meeting should always end with participants having a plan. It doesn't have to be a grandiose, twelve-point plan, but every participant should be able to articulate what the plan is moving forward as well as the agreed-on timeline to take those next steps. Personally, I respond very well to having a deadline, which helps keep me on track. As Rita Mae Brown famously said, "If it weren't for the last minute, nothing would get done" (Goodreads, n.d.b).

I was once part of a grade-level team where, at the end of the meeting, each member wrote his or her immediate next step on a post-it note. We then passed all of the notes around in a circle until we got ours back. After seeing what everyone else wrote, we could revise our next steps as needed. We then stuck the post-it note on our desks as a reminder of what we needed to do (and to hold ourselves accountable to do it).

Similar to the opening question, having someone simply ask, "So, what's the plan?" allows everyone to focus on what actions he or she needs to take as a result of the just-concluded meeting. Those steps might not be the same for everyone in the meeting—consider closing the meeting with a quick *whip around* where everyone quickly states the next step he or she is going to take as a result of what the team discussed.

Reward Creative Thought

As teachers, we not only teach for the world as it is but for the world *as it can be*. New ideas and divergent thinking are critical to our success. Collins English Dictionary Online defines divergent thinking as "thinking in an unusual and unstereotyped way, e.g. to generate several possible solutions to a problem" ("Divergent thinking," n.d.). There are ways to incentivize this kind of thinking.

Consider giving out a Divergent Thinker Award each month or semester to the meeting attendee who has come up with the most innovative ideas or who has been instrumental in seeing a new idea come to fruition. Although the meeting leader can give the award out, I've found it's more effective (and fun) when the group discusses and selects a winner together. It also allows team members to recognize and compliment one another, which helps build a positive team culture. This award sends out a clear message: we are holding these meetings so we can evolve as a group.

This evolution happens through creativity, not just standard discussion about the same old issues. In addition, the opportunity to bring in a fresh idea will get people thinking about new ideas when they are away from the meetings—a sure sign that the meetings are productive!

Invite Guests From Time to Time

Let's be honest—when you know in advance that another professional is coming in to observe you teaching, don't you try harder? Perhaps you tidy up the room a bit beforehand or dress a little nicer that day. As teachers, we are proud of our work, and we love to show it off. The same concept can apply in meetings.

In addition, as teachers, we often look to liven up our curriculum by bringing in guest speakers who can offer a deeper or different perspective. Why not use the same thinking for our teacher meetings? Of course, for this strategy to be effective, don't surprise people with the guest speaker. Let your fellow teachers know in advance that he or she is attending.

Famed business leader Richard Branson (2015) regularly brings guest speakers into his company's meetings to spark ideas and generate debate, reporting once that "the variety of speakers got the group and me thinking in new, exploratory ways."

I find that participants often begin to tune out when meetings become routine. When people think they know what to expect, their minds often wander to other things. When regularly scheduled meetings begin to feel a bit mundane, invite a special guest. Perhaps include another teacher from another subject or grade level, someone who can help spark some new ideas on a challenge that your team is facing. Consider including someone who is not normally invited to these types of meetings, such as one of the clerical staff or an instructional aide who has an additional perspective to share. Not only will the normal participants want to show off their work a bit but they will hopefully do so in a manner that is organized and professional.

Inviting the occasional guest is also a great reminder that team decisions in these meetings affect more than just those who attend the meetings—they potentially have a larger-scale effect on the entire school community. Bringing in stakeholders those decisions may affect often makes them enthusiastic to attend and contribute. I find they will return to their own department meetings full of fresh ideas and perspectives to inspire their own teams.

Turn Routines Into Traditions

What's the difference between a routine and a tradition? As I think of them, a *routine* is something that we do repeatedly, either consciously or subconsciously. A *tradition* is something special that we choose to do, often to celebrate an aspect of our culture. With traditions, a sense of family develops, and even the most mundane can become important and cherished. Stop and consider how you can make this shift in thinking in your own group. Can you add a prop or ritual to something seemingly dull—like weekly check-ins or student progress reports—to bring either some levity or deeper meaning? Can you come up with a team cheer? What if you made one meeting a month a bring-breakfast meeting during which you take twenty minutes to eat together and share your successes?

It may sound trivial, but creating traditions brings people together, encourages them to feel connected, and reminds us why we do what we do.

Summary

As professionals, we hold meetings to exchange ideas, disseminate information, and create a culture of collaboration within our organization. As educators, we embody the commitment inherent to our role by inspiring in our students the pride and confidence to make this world a better place.

We're always going to have full plates as teachers, and we're always going to have meetings. With effective, innovative, positive, and productive meetings aimed ultimately at helping our students—we're doing all this together.

Reflection Questions

Now that you have completed the chapter, consider and reflect on the following questions.

1. Think back to the last meeting you attended. What did your team accomplish? What did it fail to accomplish? How did you feel as you left that meeting?

2. Name a problem that you and your colleagues have been struggling with. How could you use divergent thinking to generate several possible solutions to the problem? How would you benefit from finding a creative solution that works?

3. Who at your school site would benefit from attending one of your next meetings, and what might he or she be able to contribute so that everyone attending could benefit? (Get creative in who you might be able to invite!)

4. What traditions have you incorporated, or could you start incorporating, into your meetings to further develop a sense of family?

WELCOME TO TEACHING. PLEASE STAY

Help Your School's New Teachers Succeed (and Stick Around)

For many schools, retaining good teachers is a considerable challenge. Retaining great teachers is a feat that requires remarkable leadership and a school culture that facilitates their success.

Consider Brenda, one of the most promising new teachers our school had ever seen. Her student teaching with students at risk got glowing reviews, she was eager to jump right into leadership roles, and her classroom was well-organized and ready days before veteran teachers had even set foot on campus.

Weeks into her first teaching year, though, she pulled me aside to tell me she felt that the staff did not want to connect with her. One colleague had even told her there was no point investing time into first-year teachers because most of them left. "Once you show up for your second year, you'll be treated like you belong here," the colleague told her.

We've all heard the dismal teacher turnover numbers, such as the National Education Association's (n.d.) calculation that 20 percent of new teachers leave the classroom within three years, and nearly 50 percent of new teachers in urban districts leave within the first five years. And we know the consequences: beyond the cost of replacing each teacher who leaves (which is estimated anywhere from $15,000 to $20,000 in large districts like Chicago [Barnes, Crowe, & Schaefer, 2007]), there is also the toll on staff morale, student confidence, and test scores.

It is imperative that we teachers look at our own personal responsibility in these statistics and recognize when we foster a culture that inhibits teacher retention. Let's ask ourselves: "Am I doing all I can to help new teachers at my school succeed? Or, am I contributing to their departure by ignoring or belittling them?"

Imagine the positive effect we could have on our schools—and ultimately the success of our students—if each of us made it a personal goal to help our schools' new teachers feel welcome, invest in the job, and stay on board. In this chapter, I present four strategies you can use to accomplish this.

Strategies for Success

Have you been looking to do more to welcome and encourage new teachers? Here are four easy ways to start.

Minimize Negative Talk

I still remember the uncomfortable, embarrassed feeling I had when I was sitting in the teachers' lounge my first year and a group of veteran teachers began to lambaste the district Beginning Teacher Support and Assessment program for inducting new teachers into the profession. One by one, they fired off a round of cynical comments about the program's uselessness. Comments such as "That's where they teach you a bunch of stuff you already learned about in the credential program," and "Ooh, more meetings when you're already swamped" filled the lounge and hovered above us like a black cloud.

I actually loved the program, felt I was learning a lot, and wanted to share some of the insights from our latest guest speaker at the next staff meeting. Guess whether I did after that teachers' lounge experience.

I know schools have a lot of issues, and the longer we staff members are there, the more familiar we are with those issues, and the more likely we are to complain about them. But we have to be smart about how we approach these criticisms. Try to refrain from badmouthing the administration, fellow teachers, programs, and students in front of new teachers. This doesn't mean being fake or keeping new teachers out of the loop—but give them a chance to be excited, bring a fresh energy to the table, and form their own opinions before you impose your weathered ones.

Often, you may find it is them exposing you to a new perspective about your school that you hadn't considered.

On the other hand, helping new teachers understand what is a normal part of the profession (and what isn't) can also go a long way. A little humor about the issues at your school can work wonders for a new teacher's perspective. Oh, the relief I felt my first semester when fellow teachers were joking about certain student behaviors I had assumed were happening only in my classroom!

In short, when it comes to the challenges of our profession and helping new teachers thrive, levity works much better than negativity.

Celebrate Milestones and Successes

Getting through the first week of school may not be a big deal to you now, but remember what an accomplishment it was your first year?

Take a few minutes to walk into the new teachers' classrooms and notice what they are doing. Acknowledge their seemingly small milestones—the first month, the first back-to-school night, the first parent conferences—and you help not only motivate them, but you open the door to asking them how things are going and if they need anything.

Whether you are praising high first test scores or a new teacher's calm handling of a student scuffle, call out new teachers' triumphs in staff meetings as well. Consider making a ritual of celebrating one new teacher's accomplishment at each department or professional development meeting. You could even come up with a funny name for it, such as a Groovy Newbie Award.

There's a larger reward in doing this as well. If you honor new teachers publicly for their successes, you not only boost morale but also set an example of teamwork and support that they will likely emulate, adding a positive vibe to your staff meetings for years to come. By helping new teachers in encouraging ways through that tough first year, you are also helping your own experience as a staff member in the future and helping build a culture where everyone grows and students succeed.

Include New Teachers in Decision Making (But Don't Force It)

One year, my mathematics department received a $400 grant, and we weren't sure what to spend it on. (At the time, it felt like a lot!) After we hemmed and hawed for a while, a new teacher spoke up and described a teaching tool he had seen at a conference. It sounded amazing. We looked into it and ultimately ended up using the grant to purchase it. I still remember the smile on the new teacher's face when we listened to his idea.

It's easy to ignore a new teacher who brings up an issue or question we've heard a million times before, and it's normal to struggle with taking a colleague seriously who's only slightly older than your students, but try to remember when you were in those new-teacher shoes and how much it meant (or would have meant) when you were included as a peer.

So, before you roll your eyes at the neophytes, open your ears; they just may surprise you with a great idea or insight. New teachers, especially the younger ones, are the most technologically savvy generation to enter the workforce. They are also the closest in age to our students, and thus, they are often the most knowledgeable about the trends and issues that affect our students. In addition, fresh out of their teacher training programs, they haven't formed any bad habits and have the benefit of being exposed to the newest ideas in teacher education. By welcoming and valuing them, we open our own learning to so many possibilities.

This is not to say you should completely remove the training wheels by forcing new teachers into jobs they can't yet handle. We all know how tempting it is to throw first-year teachers to the wolves by sticking them with the worst volunteer or leadership duties, but putting them in charge of the notoriously rowdy first dance is not a way to boost their confidence or help them survive their first year. Overwhelming new teachers can create a toxic school culture that can often result in them deciding to leave the school or the profession. Letting them get involved at their own pace and engage in duties that play to their strengths benefits everyone.

Help New Teachers Stay Healthy

The first month of my first year of teaching, each night I scarfed down a drive-through burrito for dinner after leaving school at 8:00 p.m. Then, a fellow teacher invited me to join him for an after-school surf on Thursdays (San Diego's equivalent of the East Coast racquetball date). I began looking forward to our surf session all week because I felt so much better the day of and after it, and I saw how I could actually leave school in the daylight and take care of myself now and then.

I've seen dozens of new teachers work themselves into sickness from the pressure of that first year on the job. As a veteran teacher, you can help break this kind of toxic cycle by noticing when new teachers look unwell, mention headaches or stomachaches, or have frequent doctor's appointments. Try to encourage them to give themselves a break and make their health a priority. Invite them on a weekend hike, offer them a guest pass to your gym, or bring them some fresh fruit from your backyard trees. When you show them that other teachers care about their health, they will grow to care about their own well-being too.

Also, sharing stories of how stressed out or sick you were your first year can help them feel less alone. (I threw up before school those first few days and got three colds my second semester.) Sharing how well you feel now can help them see that things do get better. (I hardly ever get the sniffles anymore, and I still try to hit the waves once a week.)

Again, there's the personal picture and the big picture; by helping an individual teacher be healthier, you also help your school. Well teachers mean fewer sick days and better teaching in general, which is what our students and our faculty teams need.

As a postscript to this strategy, I'm happy to report that Brenda—that promising new teacher—became a thriving veteran teacher. Although she succeeded despite her first-year challenges with cynical and unsupportive colleagues, many new teachers do not; they leave feeling alienated, and we all pay the price.

Summary

Each one of us can make a difference by supporting the Brendas and all the new teachers at our school. Remember when you were in their shoes, as a new teacher, and treat them as you wanted to be treated when you entered this great profession with your own dreams of helping students in great need of great teachers.

Reflection Questions

Now that you have completed the chapter, consider and reflect on the following questions.

1. Think about a new teacher you know who ended up leaving the profession after only a year or two. What were the reasons he or she left? What could have prevented him or her from leaving?

2. Does your school or district have a new teacher induction program? If so, how do most veteran teachers regard it? What can you do to help improve its perception or impact?

3. What milestones could you celebrate with your new teachers, and how could you celebrate them in a positive and creative way? Consider developing a calendar or plan to create some consistency each year.

4. What are some activities that you could include a new teacher in to help him or her stay healthy? In what ways would this improve his or her overall well-being and benefit his or her students?

TALKING 'BOUT MY GENERATION

Improve Schools by Minding Collegial Generation Gaps

Just as there are generational gaps between teachers and students, so too are there gaps between generations of teachers. Although teaching is a profession that has us working shoulder to shoulder with colleagues across several generations, we often ignore this. Or, we focus on the voids each generation brings to the table rather than the strengths that can fill those voids.

In a time when our profession is filled with volatility that comes in the form of uncertain budgets and pink slips, there is often a division between long-standing teachers with many years in the same classroom and newer teachers who have spent the past few years bouncing from job to job.

When I was invited to give a presentation at one of our district's elementary schools about a new computerized assessment program, I arrived at the school site and the principal told me, "My staff is comprised mostly of veteran teachers who are not very comfortable with computers. In fact, we can't even get some of them to check their email."

Sure enough, as I gave the presentation, I noticed the few young teachers quickly absorbing and applying the information, while the veteran teachers sat, arms crossed, looking bewildered. I left the site with a newly defined challenge before me: How do I turn that generation gap into an asset for *all* teachers and students?

In this chapter, I explain why it's critical that we openly explore and embrace generation gaps between teachers and then demonstrate how to recognize where those gaps lie and what our places on the generational spectrum tend to say about us. I then provide three strategies for making generational diversity within your school an asset, so everyone benefits.

Generational Gaps and the Importance of Talking About Them

Newsflash: we need to change the way we think, and talk, about the generation gaps among teachers.

Like many issues of diversity, minding generational gaps between teachers is something we may find hard to talk about, and it often seems easier to focus on what divides us rather than what can bring us together. But what would happen if we actually discussed this issue head-on? What if we focused on what these groups of teachers can offer one another rather than allow the generation gap to grow, which only hurts us *and* our students?

Here's what I know: when it comes to helping *one student*, nothing is more critical than the relationship between the teacher and the student. However, when it comes to helping *an entire school*, I believe nothing is more critical than the relationships between the adults in the building.

Transforming teachers' generational differences into a staff's strength (one that can help generations of students) requires a real understanding of generational issues, and some creative solutions, which you can help implement no matter where you teach.

Although exact years may vary from report to report, there are generally five generations currently at work in our schools and offices—which is a first in American history (Salzman, 2017). This can be an amazing opportunity for all of us. Simply naming these generational groups can begin to shed light on how we can all work better together.

In general, the five working generations you'll find in many schools include the following (Salzman, 2017).

1. **The traditionalists:** Also known as *the silent generation*, the traditionalists were born between 1925 and 1945 and experienced such formative

events as the Great Depression, World War II, and the postwar suburban American Dream. Although the traditionalists still working in our schools are increasingly scarce, they often still serve in volunteer positions and are a valuable resource for our students. One elementary school that I worked at runs a very effective program called Everyone a Reader, where retired volunteers sit with reluctant readers, encouraging and coaching them to improve their skills. It's wonderful!

2. **The baby boomers:** Born between 1946 and 1964, and our nation's largest generation, the formative events in baby boomers' lives included the dawn of television, rock 'n' roll, the Vietnam War, and the 1960s. This is a generation that is beginning to retire and will continue to in the years to come. Many boomers hold the institutional memory of our schools and educational system and can add valuable insight into teaching trends that have come and gone and how we can all apply those lessons to newer initiatives.

3. **Generation X:** Born between 1965 and 1980, the gen Xers grew up in a time that included the introduction of MTV and the personal computer, the explosion of the Challenger space shuttle, and the Gulf War. Unintimidated by technology, and with a couple decades of experience working in schools now under their belts, Gen Xers are well-positioned to take on leadership roles both in and out of the classroom.

4. **The millennials:** Also referred to as *gen Y* or *gen next*, the 80s-to-90s-born millennials are now the largest group in the modern workforce. They came of age with events such as the school shootings at Columbine and Virginia Tech, 9/11, and the dawn of the internet and information age. Masterful at utilizing and creating with technology, many millennial educators are a part of large, engaged networks that they can tap into for creative, effective solutions to the challenges they face.

5. **Generation Z:** Born in the mid-to-late 1990s through the early 2000s, this is the newest generation entering our workplaces. Gen Z joins our schools and offices in a time when social media is the norm and politics are anything but usual. Many educators refer to members of this generation as *digital natives*, people who grew up in a technology-dominated world. They bring with them unprecedented experience and savvy for the digital world, entrepreneurship, and all types of diversity, which will most certainly benefit modern students and more experienced colleagues.

With such a wide range of years on our planet and the experiences that have generally shaped each generation's thinking (and thus, approach to teaching), it is critical that our schools take the steps necessary to not only bridge the gaps between the generations but to use them as an advantage in improving our schools.

Strategies for Success

Whether you implement these in a small group (like your department) or suggest them to your principal to address schoolwide, the following strategies can get you and your colleagues started in talking about generational issues and making the most of generational diversity on our teams.

Acknowledge and Celebrate Generational Differences Openly

As you got a taste of in chapter 9 (page 69), pretending that age and cultural differences do not exist only widens the gap between generations. Naming and celebrating this range of perspectives on your staff can open doors to conversations and ideas that may never surface otherwise.

There is plenty of fascinating research that delves into the generalized personality traits that come with each generational cohort, which can be helpful as you work on this issue in your school teams. *Generations at Work* (Zemke, Raines, & Filipczak, 2013) is a great place to start, as is *Millennial Teachers of Color* (Dilworth, 2018). Both of these books address head-on the need to create a diverse workforce of millennial teachers. As long as everyone agrees up front to be mindful of stereotyping and understands that no one fits completely into these group traits, it can be a fun exercise to talk about the general strengths and challenges each generation brings to the table.

Consider having the staff all read a book on generations working together and have a discussion about it. In addition to the two books I mentioned previously in this section, I also recommend *From Boomers to Bloggers* by Misti Burmeister (2008). You can also try using fifteen minutes of three or four staff meetings (depending on the age span of your particular staff) to have each generational group offer up what it thinks its generational perspective can contribute to the team's success as a whole. Not only can this help create open, effective communication practices among the adults on campus, I've found it also leads to a more compassionate culture within your school. When students see adults working together cohesively, it sets an example for them to do the same.

Create Teams, Mentorships, and Communications That Mind the Gaps

In my experience, a lot of our professional development systems only widen the generational divide—one-way mentorships, teams that don't take generations into account, communications in only one mandated style. Think about empowering *all* generations when rethinking these systems at your school or district.

For example, instead of setting up a system in which the veteran teachers get their pick of the classes they teach, and the newest teachers fill in the gaps, create a system based on equitable distribution of students and teaching assignments. Instead of simply pairing up new teachers with veteran teachers to have the veterans teach the newbies, make it a two-way mentorship, where each has something to teach the other. Instead of choosing only one way to communicate among staff, come up with creative ways to get information out that fits the different generational styles—perhaps even creating a cross-generational communication team where one member texts, one emails, and one photocopies important announcements to various staff subgroups, based on preference.

The last time I made a doctor's appointment, the scheduler wrote the date and time on a small card, which I put in my wallet. A week before my appointment, I got an email reminding me that it was only a week away. Three days before, I received an automated phone message. Finally, the morning of my appointment, I got a text message reminder. Did I show up for that appointment? You bet. It wasn't just that I received four different reminders; it was effective because I received those reminders four different ways. As educators spanning different generations, everyone has his or her preferred method of being contacted—use this to more effectively communicate with each other!

There is no need to force all generations to conform to some other generation's way of being. With a little innovative thinking and teamwork, there are plenty of ways to respect and acknowledge generational differences that can unite rather than divide. Making these a priority creates a better learning environment for everyone, students included.

Remember the Common Goal

Finding commonalties between seemingly disparate groups is always beneficial in helping them work better together. For example, the next time I walk into a mixed-generation group of teachers to talk about computerized testing, I will first be sure to acknowledge the gift of the generational span in the room—the veterans who may better understand and can tell us about the history and reasoning behind testing in our district, and the fresh teachers who can often help us all feel more comfortable with the nature of the technological beast and how useful its data gathering can be (see chapter 6, page 45).

When you bring together teachers from across different generations, consider pairing up members from those generations, or lighten the mood by playing a little generations-based game, like putting so-called traits of each generation on the board, having teachers pick which goes with which, and then discussing how we need them all to implement this new system.

Then there is the ultimate commonality—your students. Make sure to hit hard on this because having successful students matters to *all* of the teacher generations. Whether you are a seasoned teacher who has seen it all, or a new teacher ready to change the world, you are all there because you believe in the promise of all the future generations.

It is our job to help our students learn and thrive, and to do this, we must pool all of our strengths and never lose sight of this shared and fundamental goal of the work we do.

Summary

One important idea I've learned from working with colleagues from different generations is that our generational culture stays with us, so we will never truly grow into understanding or being like the generations before us. In other words, a baby boomer at age twenty-five was very different than a millennial at age twenty-five, and they will retain this difference at their respective age fifty.

The same is true for the generational perspective of our students—their youthful selves are simply different than ours were, and they will never see the world as we do. So, it behooves us to accept and celebrate that each generation brings something unique to the table that will remain as such. Working *with* these differences serves all of us—from our individual student relationships to the overall culture of our staffs, schools, and districts.

Let's start talking about *all* of our generations as we strive to come together as colleagues, learn equally from each other, and serve students each day.

Reflection Questions

Now that you have completed the chapter, consider and reflect on the following questions.

1. Why is it important to recognize generational differences among a school's teachers? How do a generation's shared life experiences shape their outcome on teaching and learning?

2. Which of the five generations listed are you a part of? Think about the three teachers you work most closely with—which generations are they a part of? How have you benefitted from their knowledge and background?

3. Think about the entire teaching staff at your school. Which generations does it represent? (Perhaps all of them!) How has this shaped the culture of your school? What positive effects of having multiple generations are evident in your school? What negative effects are present?

4. In what ways could your school set up cross-generational mentoring so that everyone could learn new skills while fostering respect for each other and feeling empowered?

WE NEED TO TALK

Approach a Colleague
About a Conflict

When I signed on to be a full-time coach for teachers, my district administrators told me I'd be designing professional development, conducting sample lessons, and helping teachers plan and assess curriculum. Although I do all these things daily, what strikes me most is how often I'm called in to help coach a teacher on approaching a colleague with whom there is conflict or the potential for conflict.

As teachers, part of our job is to help students learn to get along, and yet I find myself constantly reminded how often we teachers need lessons in managing conflict among ourselves. The foundation of these lessons, I've found, is to look more deeply into the concept of conflict itself. In this chapter, I will help you rethink the nature of conflict between colleagues and offer an eight-step strategy for resolving conflicts.

How to Rethink Your Approach to Conflict

Conflict is not always a negative. It can be a positive catalyst to push us into new growth. For any successful organization, conflict is inextricably linked to those turning points that lead to success (La Duke, 2016).

Unfortunately, for an organization that is flailing, inability to deal with conflict is usually at the root of its problems. This is particularly bad for teachers, because we can't afford to let our own inability to handle conflict negatively affect our focus on the critical job at hand—educating our students.

Our students come from many different walks of life, some entering our classrooms with the weight of the world on their shoulders. The last thing they need is a teacher who is distracted by adult conflicts instead of focused on being the best teacher he or she can be.

In schools, conflict between two adults can build up over years, as some teachers stay at the same school site (even in the same classroom) for decades. In their book *The Power of Teacher Teams*, Vivian Troen and Katherine Boles (2012) state:

> It's easy to avoid conflicts by never confronting serious issues and to achieve harmony by simply allowing only the more dominant members to have a voice in conversations. Yet successful teams do not shy away from conflict; rather, they understand that there are benefits to be gained from conflict resolution. (pp. 16–17)

With most schools placing an increased emphasis on collaboration, professional development, and learning teams, many teachers who are most comfortable in their classrooms find themselves drawn out of them and into meetings where communication often goes awry. This ends up leaving the adults angry, bewildered, and unsure how to approach their colleagues to resolve issues, let alone address how those issues might affect their instructional practices.

I see this changing dynamic, which pushes teachers to deal with their own conflicts, as *a great opportunity* for all of us. The better we become at handling challenging situations with one another, the better we become at handling the challenging situations our students face. We also have the chance to truly practice what we preach in learning to get along with one another. Jennifer Abrams (2009) writes in her book *Having Hard Conversations*, "As teachers, we know we must both support and challenge students to help them grow. We need to also employ a healthy balance of both support and challenge when working with our colleagues" (p. 2).

I actually enjoy the conflict coaching I've been doing with teachers, as I love to see the light bulb turn on in teachers' eyes when they realize how easy it can be to handle a troubling situation with a colleague and use it to create a positive outcome for both parties. Rarely do I see more valuable growth occur among individuals and staff teams than when they productively and positively address conflict.

Strategies for Success

The eight strategies in this chapter work together to form a step-by-step method that any teacher can use to approach a colleague in a way that is professional, respectful, and ultimately beneficial for the relationship—and thus for the rest of the staff and students as well.

Be Well-Rounded

Whatever the nature of the conflict, think about the situation from at least three different perspectives: yours, your colleague's, and the students'. Whatever the situation is that you need to confront, thinking about it from multiple perspectives will help you see the situation more fully and will help you begin to pinpoint exactly what the issues are.

As you analyze the situation, it can be quite helpful to write down the following.

- What I need

- What my colleague needs

- What students need

For example, I once needed to approach a colleague who would sometimes make rude comments about some of our students during our grade-level meetings, often derailing the conversation. I jotted down the following.

> **What I need:** To have our department get through meetings productively, feel positive about the work we're doing, and enjoy working with our students
>
> **What my colleague needs:** An outlet to express his frustrations
>
> **What our students need:** To feel respected by our school's teachers and to know that we care about them unconditionally

Approaching the problem this way helps you clarify your own issues, puts you in a position of empathy toward your colleague, and refocuses you on the ultimate goal of best serving your students. It also helps you step away from the drama these situations often entail and look at the situation more objectively.

Confirm Behavior Without Publicly Criticizing

Often, we wonder if a colleague's behavior is bothering others or if we're the only ones noticing. It's OK to privately ask another colleague for his or her perspective; however, avoid going to him or her to engage specifically in complaint or criticism.

Doing so only pushes him or her to defend the person or criticize along with you. Either way, it places your colleague in an uncomfortable position he or she did not ask for and doesn't help the situation.

Instead, remain professional and upbeat, and focus on specific behavior and how it affects the group. Explain that you are asking not to gossip, but to help improve the situation for everyone. For example, when approaching a colleague about another colleague who constantly interrupts and dominates the conversation during meetings, consider using one of the following lines.

- "I really want to approach Linda about the way she behaves in meetings, as I'm concerned that it's affecting our faculty morale and productivity. However, first I wanted to check with you to see what your perspective is on the situation."

- "I'm concerned about Linda's behavior in meetings and how it may be affecting the group. Have you or anyone on the team ever approached her about this? If you did, how did she feel about it?"

Be sure to really listen for insights you can glean—not just to validate your perspective but also to challenge or open it up. After hearing your colleague's input, politely end the conversation, and let him or her know that you will inform him or her of what you decide to do.

Make an Appointment

Set up a time to talk with your colleague. It is important that this conversation takes place in a comfortable, private location with plenty of time to have it. Catching someone off guard is not only unfair; it often blocks the ability to have a conversation that is relaxed and real. This is especially true if someone needs to rush off or was planning on doing something else.

Here are ideas for making an appointment.

- Stop into your colleague's classroom right before a class begins, and say, "Hey, I was hoping to talk to you, but I know class is about to begin. When would be a good time? How about right after school (or at break, lunch, or so on) today?"

  This gives your colleague plenty of advance notice, which he or she had a decision in, and signals that a conversation is coming. This is also something you can email in advance if you aren't able to get to his or her class or office.

- In the event that the conversation needs to happen now, you can still begin by saying, "Hey, I need to talk to you. Is now a good time?" If it is not a good time, trust that he or she will let you know when a better time would be. Otherwise, when your colleague agrees that now is a good time, he or she has a moment to collect himself or herself and at least has had a say in the meeting taking place at that moment.

Rehearse and Open With Confidence

When you approach a colleague about a conflict, it's important that you are not "ummming" your way through the first part of the conversation. Coming in unprepared diminishes both your professionalism and the focus on finding a solution that ultimately benefits everyone.

Sometimes, knowing how to begin the conversation is the hardest part. Rehearsing a clear opening is key to whether the conversation becomes productive or gets derailed before it even begins. Consider practicing the following lines to open up the conversation.

- "I'd like to talk to you about _____. You don't have to agree with everything I say, but I do ask you to please listen first."
- "I've really been thrown off by a few things that I've seen (or heard), and I wanted to take this opportunity to address them."

Be Specific

Whenever possible, avoid making general, blanket statements about an issue; rather, use specific examples. Was the colleague twelve minutes late to the meeting yesterday? Tell him or her specifically about the twelve minutes. Did the colleague say something offensive in the staff lounge? Quote specifically what he or she said. Only when we are willing to confront someone with specifics can we hope to address and improve the specific behavior.

Always keep in mind when addressing conflict that it is imperative that we separate behavior from self-worth. Telling someone that he or she came to the meeting late (behavior) is far more productive than telling that individual that he or she *never* gets anywhere on time (self-worth). Remember that as uncomfortable as it might seem to confront someone, it is often even more uncomfortable to be confronted.

Your colleague might get defensive, embarrassed, or angry. Stay calm, keep a relaxed posture, and just take some breaths. Tell him or her that you're here to work this out and proceed to the next step.

Be Real and Listen

As Susan Scott (2017) writes in her best-selling book, *Fierce Conversations*, "Authenticity is not something you have; it is something you choose" (p. 82). It's OK to laugh, to cry, or to admit to being confused during a conversation. It's also OK if the conversation goes silent for a few moments. By bringing our authentic selves into a conversation, it enables us to lean *into* a conflict instead of shying away from it.

Confronting a colleague does not mean that you do all the talking. Actually, after you have opened the conversation with your specifics, the majority of what you should be doing is *listening*. Listen to understand your colleague's perspective with a goal of finding solutions. Avoid fabricating your responses from the moment she opens her mouth. (This is not listening!)

However, this doesn't mean letting your colleague turn you into a dumping ground for his or her issues and problems either. Part of being real is knowing your healthy boundaries and when a conversation is not going well.

Should the conversation begin to go badly or in circles, feel free to pause and commit to coming back to the issue later. If necessary, tell your colleague that you feel the conversation is not going well and that you feel your next step should be to call in an administrator or mediator.

Make a Plan

Conclude the conversation by agreeing on a plan of action, including how you will hold each other accountable. Too often, great meetings conclude with everyone feeling better, but with no plan in place for effecting future change. This greatly increases the chances of the problem occurring again.

Simply saying, "So, what's the plan?" moves the conversation toward implementable solutions that propel the cause forward. Once you have a plan all parties agree on, make it official by writing it down, including specific steps for achieving the outcome you all desire.

Of course, there might be times when there isn't an immediately actionable plan you and your colleagues can make. Maybe the situation is escalating to an undesirable place? In these cases, it's okay to pause the conversation and mutually agree to take a few days to reflect on it or make time to bring in other people (if necessary). Whatever the outcome, just make sure to do what you agree to!

Appreciate and Follow Up

In the days and weeks after the conversation ends, be sure to let your colleague know how much you appreciate working with him or her. Follow up on your action plan. Depending on the nature of the conversation, consider asking your colleague how he or she is feeling, or if he or she has had any further thoughts since you concluded.

You will have to use your professional judgment to decide how often and to what degree to bring up the issue. Going overboard can escalate matters rather than bring about positive resolution. The greatest indication of the conversation's success is whether the conflict is ultimately resolved and everyone involved is able to productively move forward.

Summary

Our students are counting on us to be at our best each day. To do this, we need to proactively and professionally handle the conflicts that inevitably arise when human beings work together.

If we see our own workplace conflicts as natural, and as opportunities for growth, we can address them calmly and positively. This helps our teams, and our schools, best serve the students who need us.

Reflection Questions

Now that you have completed the chapter, consider and reflect on the following questions.

1. On a scale of 1–10 (1 being very poor, and 10 being perfect), how would you rate your ability to handle conflict? How would you rate your school, overall, at handling conflict? What changes can you make in your own handling of conflict to create better outcomes?

2. Think about an issue or situation at your school that caused conflict in the past. What, if anything, did the involved parties do to resolve it? Which of the eight steps I present in this chapter could have improved the process of addressing the conflict?

3. Of the eight steps for successful conflict resolution, which do you feel would be the most challenging for you to implement, and why? How can you meet the challenge?

4. Is there a current conflict at your school that, if resolved, would improve your school's culture? Name the conflict, then go back through the eight steps in this chapter to develop a plan to resolve it.

TURN JOB SHARES INTO WIN-WIN-WINS

Learn Five Ways to Make Shared Positions Work for Teachers, Students, and Administrators

This chapter was coauthored with Megan Pincus-Kajitani.

Job sharing is a practice in which two teachers share a single position, including its benefits, work hours, and responsibilities. It's not a practice that all schools engage in, but in those that do, it can be of great benefit for teachers who need to split their time between teaching and some other aspect of life such as going back to school, providing childcare or taking care of a family member, or attending to a health issue. At the same time, it can also present unique challenges for students, teachers, and administrators.

While participating in a meeting about some staff issues at a school site, a principal told me that after her first year leading the school's staff, she abolished all job shares. She felt job shares were great for the two teachers, but not necessarily so for their students. According to this principal, job shares—or the agreement between two teachers to share one contracted teaching position by coming in on different

Special thanks to the job-sharing teachers in the Escondido Union School District who contributed their wisdom to this chapter, especially Mrs. Jennifer Byers and Mrs. Jenny Rhoades, whose expertise and experience are making a positive impact on the students they teach every single day!

days—were ineffective, confusing for the students, and did not promote the highest levels of student learning. She stated that it is her duty to ensure the learning of all students, which includes making tough decisions, such as the one to disallow job shares at her site.

As I left the meeting, I couldn't help thinking that while this decision might make things seem easier in the short term, or even boost test scores for a year or two, overall, it hurts our society.

First, it forces working parents (who occupy most job shares) into an all-or-nothing decision regarding choosing between parenting full-time or teaching full-time. Second, it stifles the kind of creative thinking, relationship building, and flexibility that we *all* need to learn (adults *and* youth) to thrive in the workplaces of the future.

I kept asking myself, "Isn't there a way we can offer the flexibility of job shares to teachers and have students succeed at the same time? Aren't there job shares that work? What will it take to find a win-win here?"

So, I decided to do a little research by speaking with job-sharing teachers around our school district about what was working for them and what was not. I also talked with principals about what they saw, both good and bad.

After identifying the pitfalls that ineffective job shares seem to fall victim to, I also pinpointed cases in which the job shares were working. I found several instances where two teachers worked together quite harmoniously and to great benefit to their students. Those students now had two effective teachers, who were looking out for their best interests each day. From these conversations, I came up with some concrete ideas for creating a win-win for teachers and students—*and* a win for administrators as well.

Strategies for Success

In the following sections, I present five strategies for creating and maintaining effective job shares that will allow *teachers* the work-life balance they deserve, *students* the high level of achievement that they are entitled to, and *administrators* a smoother ride in managing job-share teams.

Plan in Advance

Most teachers return to work the week before the students begin their first day in the fall. Getting the room ready, attending meetings, making copies, and prepping first-week activities are usually the norm. However, for two teachers who will share a classroom and the same students, the regular prep week prior to school starting is too late to be shaking hands with your partner for the first time. Effective job shares are ones that everyone involved plans *the school year prior*. This gives you and your participating teacher time to get used to each other and plan ahead.

Whenever possible, you and your soon-to-be partner should go and observe each other in action in your classrooms. Get to know your partner's teaching style, communication style, educational philosophy, and supply closet.

Sit down and set some goals together, brainstorm ideas, or create a job-share mission statement. Then divide up some homework (to address the questions in the fourth strategy, Put It in Writing, page 148), and make some planning dates during summer so you, as a duo, can arrive in the fall feeling dynamic, comfortable with one another, and prepared.

Drop the Attitude

A teaching partnership is much more than the merging of two personalities (although that is a piece of it)—it is the merging of two sets of supplies, two sets of expertise, and two sets of prior experiences. It is likely both teachers come in with similar grade-level and subject-matter experience. Although this can be a good thing from which a partnership draws strength and effectiveness, conflict could also arise when one colleague or the other decides his or her ideas are inherently better. When this happens, use the strategies I provide in chapter 18 (page 137).

Job shares that work feature two teachers who choose to drop the egos, scrap any thoughts of competition, and agree to cooperate, support one another, and encourage success as individuals and as a team—this ultimately means student success.

As we often ask of our students, insist on being a lifelong learner. Be forthright regarding the strengths and weaknesses that you are bringing into the partnership. Your partner's weakness is yours as well (and vice versa), so look for solutions that will help you both and that ultimately benefit your students. The goal is to adapt and adopt, rather than outperform your partner teacher. When one of you wins, you both win, and students win—the same goes for losing.

In addition, take cues from your students about areas in which you can improve as a team. When a student says, "Ms. X doesn't do it that way," this is a perfect chance to identify areas in which you and your colleague are not effectively communicating.

When a student says this, don't assign blame on your partner teacher; rather, see it as a normal part of this kind of arrangement—and an opportunity to improve your duo's communication and work cooperatively together to find solutions. Think of the example this sets for students about effective partnership and leadership in the process.

Begin and End the Year Together

On the first day of school, it is crucial that both teachers be present in the classroom. This gives the students the important message that there is no one teacher that is really in charge (even if one will be there more days). Present the situation as a benefit to the students by explaining to them that they are members of only a few classes (or the only class) that get to have two teachers!

In addition, spend some time on the first day explaining to the students *why* you have both chosen to participate in this job share. It is important for students to see that adults—especially the well-educated adults that we desire them to be one day—have work options, take those work options seriously, and are capable of prioritizing their own children as well as the students they teach.

Be sure to explain to students how you will be communicating with your partner teacher throughout the school year. Along with the obvious methods of phone calls, emails, and texting, show them the journal that you will be leaving for each other, as well as what you'll be communicating about. An effective journal will include student and parent updates, assignments due, unfinished work, and so on. Perhaps you will also introduce a class website together, where both teachers will interact with students and parents.

Just as you begin the first day of school together, it is equally important to finish the last day of school together. This sends a clear message to your students that you continue to care deeply for them all the way through to the end. It also sends a message about what teamwork means, and it's an excellent opportunity to make contact with parents, many of whom show up on the last day of school to pick up their children and say goodbye.

Put It in Writing

Let's be honest—sometimes the day-to-day grind of being a teacher results in us loosening our grip a bit on the procedures and routines that make our classrooms function smoothly. This is understandable, but with job shares, this poses a particular challenge, especially when one teacher holds to the routines and the other one doesn't.

This is why job-share partners must work extra hard at setting and keeping consistent classroom procedures throughout the school year. Pull out that copy of *The First Days of School* (Wong & Wong, 2009) from your credential program, and read it in tandem as soon as you sign your job-share agreement in the spring. As job sharers, it is critical that you put these kinds of procedures in place from day one, put them in writing, and stick to them.

Visibly posting the classroom procedures, routines, and expectations and training students to recognize that what is posted is the law of the land can help avoid the uncertainty that can often occur in the absence of these being highly visible. In addition, create checklists or a handbook that includes what each teacher will agree to do during the day, at the end of each day, and the day before the other partner teacher's designated days begin.

A teacher should never walk into the classroom wondering what it will look like or where something is. Moreover, try to help your colleague begin the day with a clear lesson plan, and avoid leaving your partner teacher a pile of stuff to deal with (the ungraded papers you didn't quite get to, paperwork that still needs to be filled out, or samples you've been meaning to hang on the wall).

Finally, get down to the nitty-gritty. How will you display work throughout the classroom? How will you have students format homework papers? What exact words and phrases will you use to discipline and reward students? Showing solidarity is often the result of doing lots of little things the same way.

Of course, you will adjust as you learn, but aiming for consistency from the start will greatly help you. When your administrators experience the benefits of having two content job-share partners and successful, secure students, paying attention to these details will pay off tremendously.

Set (Flexible) Limits

Remember, for many, the goal of a job share is to balance the high demands of being a parent (or carry the weight of some other major responsibility) *and* a teacher. Sometimes this results in a parent who spends too much time thinking about what is happening in the classroom and a teacher who feels guilty for not being at home. Instead of allowing you to focus equally on dual roles, this can make you ineffective in both. Teachers in a job share need to be focused on the responsibilities that are in front of them on that particular day. Acknowledge this, and work to find balance and boundaries together. Set limits on when you'll talk, email, or text—knowing these limits are for the benefit of everyone.

Yes, there are times when instant and frequent communication is critical; however, resist the urge to be in constant contact. I've seen job-sharing teachers texting their partners during their entire lunch period, which is a recipe for double burnout.

While having both teachers attend events such as back-to-school night or certain performances shows solidarity, it is not always necessary for both teachers to attend everything together. A successful job-share team I interviewed actually staggered their parent conferences in separate areas of the classroom, so both were visible but met with parents separately. Be strategic in your planning!

Of course, there are times when flexibility is key to uphold consistency for students. For example, if one teacher knows she is going to be out sick or attending a training, it is much more effective to have the partner teacher in the classroom on that particular day instead of calling in a substitute. In this scenario, consider trading days in order to keep the students on the path of truly effective learning.

Summary

Let's be realistic: when principals like the one I spoke with (who banned job shares) are doubtful of the positive potential of this workplace practice, it is up to job sharers to go the extra mile to show how effective job shares can be. Yes, as a part-time job sharer, you may have to plan ahead more, communicate more, and decide things in advance more than a typical full-time classroom teacher, but isn't it worth it for the flexibility?

The extra advance work will benefit everyone in the long run, creating more security in the classroom environment for all and less work as the year progresses when your systems are running smoothly.

There may be a time when as many men as women are sharing jobs more, and sharing parenting more, which I bet many of you would applaud. To make this happen for all of us, though, we need to put in the time and effort now to make job shares cooperative for teachers, and above all, effective for student learning.

Win-win-win job shares *are* possible with proper planning and communication, and I challenge every school district to rise to the occasion and show our students this positive example of work-life balance and teacher teamwork!

Reflection Questions

Now that you have completed the chapter, consider and reflect on the following questions.

1. Have you had any experiences with participating in a job share? If so, what worked well, and what did not?

2. What do you see as the biggest challenges with convincing an administrator that a job share is beneficial to both teachers and all students? What work can you do in advance to address these challenges?

3. Once in a job share, in what ways could you communicate your successes (and challenges) to your administrators and parents to show it is working?

4. When working in a job share, what collaborative challenges or conflicts have arisen with your partner teacher? Were you able to successfully overcome them? If not, how could you improve your conflict-resolution practices to produce better outcomes?

PART 4

Owning It in Your Community: Strategies for Making a Positive Impact Beyond Your School and Classroom

THE GENERAL PUBLIC ON TEACHERS

Turn Potential Foes Into Supportive Allies

One thing teachers find, whenever we leave the comfort of our campuses, is that many members of the public seem to have strong opinions about what education should look like. Often these opinions come from their own politics or experiences they had when they were in school. Regardless of the source, this means people also tend to have strong opinions about teachers, and often, those opinions lack a true understanding of what we do all day (and at night, and on weekends, and over summer "vacations").

Here is an example: One spring day, I was pushing my daughter on the swing at our local park. As happens often, the dad pushing the swing next to me and I began chatting, and eventually, talk turned to our jobs. As soon as I said that I am a teacher, the conversation turned to the popular headlines. Yes, he had heard a news report on the state of education and was now convinced that the teacher unions are to blame for our country's education woes—along with bad teachers and tenure. Suddenly, I became the spokesperson for all bad teachers, all union decisions, and a system that awards tenure too easily.

As teachers, we are often too busy, and too engaged in helping our students succeed, to stop and pay attention to the headlines. We are certainly often too preoccupied to stop and defend the teaching profession to those who consider themselves experts on schools because, once upon a time, they attended them.

Whether this talk comes from the media, politicians, or a casual playground conversation, it's tempting to fight back and defend our work, even when we lack the resources and training to do so. In this chapter, I write about the importance of understanding that all people form an opinion on topics, regardless of their personal knowledge or experience, and then dive straight into five strategies you can use to help ensure the people in your community are your allies, not your foes. They might even become true advocates for the work we do.

All People Have Opinions—About Everything

Consider the classic example of when Oprah badmouthed beef eating on her show. The cattle farmers defended themselves vigorously, taking out full-page ads in major newspapers, taking her to court, and even managing to land themselves on many a late-night talk show, making Oprah jokes as the general public laughed along (Verhovek, 1998).

Whatever you might feel about that story, for our purposes, it's important to understand one key attribute of it—most people know very little about what goes into cattle farming. Why would they? That doesn't stop them from having opinions about it, because it's all too human for people to have opinions about pretty much anything and everything. The same is true of classroom teaching. This makes the best way to fight back not to raise the level of rancor, but to productively engage in conversations about our profession with people who can ultimately better shape and inform the opinions of others.

Strategies for Success

The following five strategies can help you make allies of the general public—whether you are at a cocktail party or on a playground—by helping them get more informed about the realities of our profession and realize that teaching is one of the most rigorous, most profound, and most important jobs in the world.

Stop Reading the News, and Start Creating It

The next time you read an education-related story in your local newspaper or magazine, take notice of the author. Often, an email address will accompany the article, especially in the online version. Keep these addresses on file, and the next time your classroom, school, or district is doing something newsworthy, email or call to let the reporter know. Before you do this, make sure to find out what your school or district's guidelines are on speaking with the media and inviting them into your classroom. Most of the time, district leaders love positive news about something happening in their community!

You can also call your local paper and ask who its education reporter is. Often, reporters are under contract to write ten or so stories per week, and they are looking for things to write about. Furthermore, the way the internet and news often work, small, local stories sometimes turn into statewide or even national news. Once you find out who that reporter is, don't contact him or her blindly. Make sure to read some of the previous stories the reporter has written. Observe his or her reporting style and take note whether the individual provides coverage that is well-researched, balanced, and generally treats educators in a positive light, or at least fairly.

A positive news story about the work we are doing also gives it a sense of legitimacy and importance that can help sway public opinion in our favor. Be sure to give the stories a wider reach and a longer life by sharing the good news on your school or class website or blog and on social media!

Tell Stories

Stories are powerful. They create connection and context and often drive people's emotions and opinions when all the data in the world does not. Powerful stories have an immediate and lasting effect and can convince even the most skeptical of the important work that teachers do.

Note that when I say, "Tell stories," I don't mean something from your own childhood, but about the realities that students and schools face every day. I once told a friend about a student who, after our promotion ceremony on the last day of school, refused to leave early, insisting that he stay for lunch. After much prodding and questioning from me, he finally yelled, "I just want to eat lunch one more time before I go home all summer to nothing!"

A few days later, my friend told me that he couldn't stop thinking about the story I had told him and couldn't get the image of the hungry student out of his head. He also realized how difficult the job of teaching is, especially teaching students who too often go hungry.

Teaching is so much more than academic content and test scores; however, this is something that the general public easily loses sight of. People can read all day long about the challenges of poverty, but the tragically real ways poverty manifests in real life are not necessarily something they see and experience firsthand. As teachers, we see and interact with students affected by poverty every day. When you use real stories to make people aware of the reality of educating students, you help them make real connections that stay with them and influence their thinking about education and the work we do.

Offer Your Podium

Let's return to the playground scenario I outlined at the start of this chapter. In the course of that conversation, I eventually had the chance to ask the dad pushing the other swing what *he* did for work. It turns out that he's a scientist. "That's incredible," I said. "You have to come in and speak to my students!"

A month later, he was standing at the front of my classroom, nervously telling thirty-two eighth graders how he spends each day. Of course, his visit to my classroom also included a tour of our campus, a lunch in our cafeteria, and a peek into the classrooms of some of our other teachers. (We explore this idea in detail in chapter 21, page 165.)

When he left, he was no longer an outsider questioning the validity of what teachers do. He was now a passionate member of the school community, ready to vigorously defend the hard work educators do each day. Everyone you meet in your community is someone who can potentially come in and share his or her experiences with your students, and the school just might gain an advocate in the process.

Look the Part

Be honest: Would you feel comfortable taking advice from a doctor who walked into your appointment in jeans and a T-shirt? Would you let a lawyer defend you in similar dress? Would you buy a car from someone in shorts and flip-flops?

As educators, many of us attain incredibly high levels of education in order to do the jobs we do, and we have every right to consider ourselves professionals. We are appalled when someone implies that we don't work hard. If all that is true, however, then shouldn't we dress accordingly?

Every day, we have an opportunity to show hundreds of students how a professional dresses, along with the barista in the coffee shop, and everyone else we come into contact with on our way to and from our office.

This isn't just about surface image but about professionalism and respect for what we do. I believe if we want the community to respect us as professionals, we must remember that how we look creates a lasting impression in the minds of those we interact with.

Brag Equally

I have to admit, I was distraught when a colleague of mine posted on her Facebook page, "Slept 'til noon, hanging at the beach. I love being a teacher on spring break."

What message does this send to our nonteacher friends and acquaintances?

One of the biggest misperceptions of the teaching profession is that we get summers off, vacations throughout the year, and only work six-hour days. The last thing we should do is give the impression that any of these fallacies are true.

Obviously, what you prefer or even need to share in a personal space is a personal decision, and I'm not advocating a gag order on sharing the benefits of the teaching profession. I'm just saying it's important to really think about the messages you are sending and how the audience you're speaking to will interpret those messages. This is important whether you're talking about teaching and education or local or national politics or how you talk about friends or family. Words have both meaning and impact, and it's important to have respect for their power. So, if you feel the need to write social media posts similar to my colleague's, consider how you might balance that out by also posting thoughts that provide your audience with a broader (and more accurate) context. For example:

> "I graded papers 'til midnight, woke up at 5:00 a.m., and finalized my lesson plan. Ready for my teaching day!"

Or how about:

> "Enjoyed my half-hour lunch. Spent fifteen minutes helping a student, and fifteen minutes eating, using the restroom, and making fifty copies."

Or maybe:

> "It was totally worth the six hours of lesson planning to see my students make the connection in class today between the civil rights movement and the recent election."

For many of us, social media is the dominant form of communication we utilize. Take advantage of this! Use it to proactively defend and realistically portray the profession we all love so much.

Summary

I look forward to the day when I see a commercial for the teaching profession during the Super Bowl, or the day when teachers stand alongside movie stars and professional athletes as some of the most visible personalities. Those may be lofty aspirations, but they derive from the reality that it is up to us as educators to spread the word about the incredibly challenging and incredibly rewarding work we do with our students, when we're in the classroom and out of it. When we do that, we make our mission more effective for everyone.

That is a concept worth "liking."

Reflection Questions

Now that you have completed the chapter, consider and reflect on the following questions.

1. Have you ever had a conversation about education with someone who works outside of education? What did you talk about, and what was the result of the conversation? Was there an opportunity to relate the high value of your teaching?

2. Has a newspaper ever run a story on you or your class, your school, or your district? Find out who wrote the story and contact him or her the next time you have something newsworthy to share. It can be a school event, a special program, or a story of success. (Make sure you know and adhere to your school or district's policies on interacting with the media.)

3. What is a story from your personal teaching experiences that highlights some of the struggles we face as educators? Consider telling this story (out loud) a few times to see how it resonates with people. Then, have it handy to tell other people whenever you need it.

4. What is a social media post that you could compose and share to better communicate the rigors of being an educator? (It could be fun and lighthearted, serious, or even gut-wrenching.)

START SPREADING THE NEWS

Put the Spotlight on Your School

Think about how often it seems like the only news people hear about education is *negative* news, and as a result, how often people assume the worst, especially when it comes to schools with large numbers of students at risk. It doesn't have to be that way.

At an annual Title I meeting for a low-performing school in our district, I happened to sit next to a parent who was clearly nervous. When I inquired, she told me she was upset because she thought the meeting meant the state was taking over the school, the teachers were going to be fired, and the school could close.

I quickly explained that Title I didn't reflect the school being at risk of a state takeover, but rather it's simply a status determined by the number of students receiving free and reduced-price lunch. When I helped her understand it was just an informational meeting, and her children's school was not at risk of state takeover, she visibly relaxed. Lack of information created fear, and when people are afraid, they find it hard to focus on anything else.

As educators and leaders working to improve the lives and futures of all our students, I firmly believe it is part of our larger responsibility to communicate what is really happening in our schools, clearly and broadly, to parents and the larger community. In this chapter, I explain how we, as teachers, are our school's best marketers and follow that up with four strategies you can use to help promote all the wonderful things about your school.

In the previous chapter, I discussed how reaching out to your local news reporter can help the general public learn about some of the wonderful things happening in our schools. In this chapter, we examine ways that we can specifically show off the work we're doing to those who want a deeper look and control the narrative about the messages we're trying to send.

We *Are* the Marketing Department

So we're supposed to be marketers now? Really? I know. We're already plenty busy doing what we're supposed to be doing—*teaching*. Our credential programs do not teach or prepare us to be public relations experts or marketing directors; however, the truth is, if we don't become savvy communicators with our schools' parents and communities, we miss opportunities to better serve our students.

I've found that clear communication with parents gives students a better chance of success, because if their caretakers feel connected with their school, students are more likely to get some support at home. Not only this, but positive press elevates the morale of everyone at a school and can be a great validating and motivating force for students who may need more encouragement about their work and potential.

Although it's true many of our districts already have a marketing professional on staff, those individuals (who are *very* helpful allies!) usually have more-than-full plates and focus on more regional communications.

So, the ball falls in our court to spread the news to our neighborhood parents and other citizens about the incredible work we're doing in our classrooms, the progress our school and students are making, and the importance of partnership opportunities that exist between a school site and the community that surrounds it.

Strategies for Success

Fostering increased engagement with your community doesn't actually take much time or money, especially if a school staff team comes together to work toward the vision of clearer and broader communication with that larger school community. Here are four low-cost ways you and your school can begin to market it and start spreading the word about what's happening at your school site.

Offer Campus Tours

One of the most effective ways to get the word out about the great things going on within your school is to bring people in to see it all firsthand. Campus tours led by someone who is well-versed in the school's mission, vision, and inner workings offer parents of prospective students, community members, and local business members a glimpse into what is happening at a school. They get to witness students and teachers hard at work, get a glimpse of curriculum as it is being taught, and ask relevant questions. If your school has something that it is especially proud of, such as interactive whiteboards, or an accomplished program, make sure the tour includes these sightings. It works particularly well to have the tours on the same day each week or month, at the same time. This ensures that everyone on campus knows that the tour is happening, can prepare accordingly, and no one gets caught off guard when the tour comes through!

Invite local business groups, Rotary Clubs, chambers of commerce, and nonprofits, and advertise at the local library, in the local newspaper, or on social media. (Don't forget to look at the chapter 20 strategy, Stop Reading the News, and Start Creating It, page 156.) Even offering a tour once a month can impact your school by bringing in community members or press to connect with the school, see what's really happening there, and feel a stake in its success.

Create a High-Quality Website

A high-quality website does not necessarily mean a high-cost website. With free websites available on sites such as Google or WordPress, any marginally tech-literate person can create a snazzy site that offers students, teachers, and parents the opportunity to stay current on everything from school events to nightly homework. Chances are, there is at least one professional on your campus who could take on website design and maintenance, perhaps as their adjunct duty.

Although most schools already have their own website, consider creating a more specialized one for your grade level, department, or specific class. That way, you can update it as often as needed, and those who visit the site will hopefully feel that they are a part of a smaller, closer-knit community. You could also start with something as simple as a Facebook page, Instagram account, or Twitter account.

Just as businesses rely on their websites to connect with customers, provide relevant information, and communicate with their clientele, schools can do the same. Make sure to create a reason for people to go to the website, such as to gain necessary information regarding an upcoming event, as an easy link to the portal to check students' grades, or to read the latest happenings as teachers blog about their classes. If you want the site you build to include a blog, I offer more strategies for getting one off the ground in chapter 24 (page 189, Five Steps to Start Your Own Blog).

Find Your Niche and Brand It

My last school had an amazing video-production program, where students at risk produced award-winning short films. Another school in the district has a phenomenal program that ensures *all* of its students master their multiplication tables. Yet another has an incredibly effective, forward-thinking principal, with a clearly stated mission to create leaders at all levels of the school.

What stands out at your school? Do people know about it? Think about what makes your school unique, in a positive way, and brand your school with these features and qualities. Make sure to highlight examples of what this looks like on your website, in your newsletters, and on social media.

If this is not immediately clear, you can come together as a staff and create a mission statement or tagline and brainstorm ideas on how to make sure the community knows about what your school stands for. Pinpoint key players from your staff who can get out into the community and speak, and find opportunities for them to spread the message you want to send about your school and who you are.

Empower Student Voices

The most powerful examples of our schools are, of course, our students themselves. Think about ways to empower them to share their successes and ideas while practicing their communication skills at the same time.

An after-school journalism club could create a simple newsletter with student-written stories for parents and community members. (Consider parents may be more likely to read something from students than from the school's adults.) Be sure to make the newsletter available on the school's website and push it out to the public via social media.

I can imagine how a student newsletter with a brief piece describing the Title I meeting would've helped the mother I described meeting at the start of this chapter feel less intimidated while also giving students an opportunity to really start talking about the issues in their community.

Over the years, I've had many members of the media visit my classroom, and my students always rose to the occasion. Prepping them for reporters who might ask them questions always gave me perfect opportunities to coach them on the crucial skills of public speaking and interpersonal communication.

I also was sure to talk to them about *why* we wanted to make a positive impression to the media—to show the world that their neighborhood was not a negative place, but one full of amazing people like them who have so much to offer the world.

Summary

Yes, marketing your school may feel like something that isn't your job, or it's just one more thing to add to your busy schedule, and I know it is easy to be cynical about public relations, the media, and all that. But think of the misinformed mother at the Title I meeting, the student whose eyes light up (and self-esteem skyrockets) when he or she sees himself or herself featured in a local news story, and the potential partnerships and support those campus-touring Rotary Club members or local press can offer to your school.

We can find real value in taking the time to work on this kind of intentionally positive communication as part of our role as teacher leaders who see the bigger picture beyond the classroom.

Reflection Questions

Now that you have completed the chapter, consider and reflect on the following questions.

1. Does your school have a website? What is the primary reason people go to the site, and how often is it updated? What information could you share on the site that would help bolster your school's image?

2. What makes *your* school unique? Develop a plan to tell others about it, and consider collaborating with other schools in the area that are doing similarly great work.

3. Does your school or district have someone in charge of communications and marketing? What are some newsworthy stories that you could tell this person about to help you get some press coverage?

4. What are some ways that you could empower students to share their voices about their school or their lives? How could you share what they create with the rest of the school and wider community?

COMMUNITY-BASED PROFESSIONAL DEVELOPMENT

Get Teachers Into the Community and the Community Into Teachers

Professional development has a critical role in developing a teacher's skills. From learning fresh strategies to differentiate our instruction to mastering a new program or technology device, good professional development keeps us collaborating, motivated, and on the cutting edge of understanding our students and how to best help them learn. Although I could go on and on about the benefits of professional development, I'm not convinced we always do the necessary work to set up professional development sessions for success.

Consider for a moment Apple. There are abundant reasons why Apple has experienced unprecedented success since the original iPod's 2001 release, but it was during a visit to a local Apple Store that I realized one of the core reasons they are so progressive and powerful as compared to our often antiquated school system (which I argue is far too stagnant).

- **Scene one:** As I walked through the Apple Store, I saw people sitting together at long tables, talking, playing with the latest techie products, and asking questions in a nonthreatening atmosphere. Some left with new goodies, some left with their current gadget fixed or upgraded, and some left empty-handed after checking out items with interest. I felt a buzz of energy, curiosity, and camaraderie among shoppers and staff.

- **Scene two:** The next day, I went to a three-hour professional development training for teachers. We were crammed into a drab room that was too small for the number of teachers there, we listened to a trainer who lectured at us, and we weren't given a break until one of the teachers in attendance spoke up and asked for it. In addition, we were all told exactly what we were expected to do when we returned to our classrooms the next day. There was barely any participation or connection. I felt a vibe of frustration, boredom, stagnancy, and isolation within the stuffy, crowded room.

A week later, I bumped into a colleague who was also at that training and asked if she had implemented the changes. She told me she hadn't and that she was actually so uncomfortable she couldn't really pay close attention and found it challenging to concentrate. As we walked off, I noticed that we were both busily looking at our iPhones. My mind flashed back to the excited atmosphere of learning that I had witnessed at the Apple Store a week earlier.

Then, it hit me—the environment and methodology for professional development matter just as much as its content and purpose. Given this, how could we make the atmosphere of our professional development meetings feel more like the Apple Store?

I saw clearly it's time for a change of scenery, a new environment and approach, one that gives our professional development a shot of energy, curiosity, and camaraderie. We need to get out of the dreary staff room and connect in new places and ways.

I've always been an advocate of neighborhood-based field trips with students to help connect us teachers with our students' communities. The crowded Apple Store–training room dichotomy led me to look into educational field trips for teachers as well, experiences to both connect us further with our students' communities and give us a shot of energy with our staff professional development frameworks.

Our school district called it *community-based professional development*, and it began implementing it in 2013. The teachers loved it! Immediately upon us advertising each experience, the available spots filled up quickly (we often had to start a waiting list), and teachers reported that they really enjoyed the opportunities to get into the community, valued experiencing their community in an authentic way, and learned several new strategies and ideas that they were able to implement in their classroom.

In this chapter, I examine the community-based professional development concept in greater detail and then explain a six-step process for developing your own community-based professional development events.

The Purpose of Community-Based Professional Development

Community-based professional development is professional development that occurs within the community that serves the students we teach. The main goal is simple: foster a stronger bond between the teachers who teach in a community and the public who lives in that community. The secondary goal is subtler, but also important: bring new life and perspective into often-dull professional development trainings for teachers.

You can hold community-based professional development sessions in a variety of locations, such as at a library, a coffee shop, or a restaurant—anywhere that teachers can get out from the traditional walls of their classroom or conference room and get into the community they serve. (Unfortunately, standing in a parking lot for twenty minutes discussing a teaching strategy can be great, but doesn't count!) A side benefit is that it gives the public in your community an opportunity to see teachers in action: planning, collaborating, and working hard to ensure the success of our students, who also happen to be their children.

In our district, we've found community-based professional development relatively easy to implement, and it has brought new life both to professional development for our staff and to our schools' connections to our community.

Strategies for Success

Anyone can organize community-based professional development. As is sometimes the case in a school district, a school in one part of town serves a completely different type of community than another school across town. With *community* being the operative word, a teacher (or group of teachers) or an administrator can organize it, hopefully in conjunction with someone in the local community, such as a shopkeeper, business or restaurant owner, or public services professional. Here are six easy strategies for planning and successfully executing a community-based professional development session.

Select a Topic and a Presenter

Although many professional development opportunities include bringing in a presenter or expert, the point of community-based professional development is not to bring outside experts in; rather, to bring *inside experts out*. Pick a topic that teachers in your school or district would like to learn about, and find an expert on that topic from within the school or district who would be willing to put together a workshop. Or, find an outside expert who is willing and able to come into your community and present in a compelling way.

Find a Location

The location you choose for your professional development doesn't have to be anywhere fancy or hip. Check to see if the local library has a spare room. Or, remember that the typical time of afternoon that teachers finish their teaching for the day happens to be the exact time that restaurants and coffee shops are at their slowest point of the day (in between the lunch and dinner crowds). Just make sure that it's a comfortable, clean space that is conducive to adult learning. (In other words, no more cramming everyone in to a drab, windowless room!)

When you identify an ideal space, find its manager or proprietor and ask if he or she would be willing to let you use the banquet room or section off a portion of space for your teacher group to gather. Remind him or her that the teachers will be purchasing coffee, drinks, or food, and that they will most likely return with their families and tell others about the great experience they had there. This is also a good time to highlight the community benefits of other patrons getting to see teachers engaged in improving learning for the community.

Many coffeehouse and restaurant owners have been in the community for a long time, probably went to school in the community where you now teach, and will be happy to help. This gives them a chance to support teachers and schools without having to make a straight donation. Of course, if they are willing to donate any food or drinks, that will only get teachers more excited about the event.

Publicize It as an Experience, Not as a Workshop

Part of making a professional development session successful is making its participants excited to be a part of it. Put in the time and effort to create a good-looking flier or web page, and get it to all the teachers who might be interested. Don't just hand them the flier and move on. Ask for a few minutes of their time so you can explain that this is a fresh way to experience professional development while connecting with each other and the community. Because our district has a wonderful technology department, we were able to make a fun video advertising some of the events and send out a link to it to potential participants. Of course, make sure to utilize social media to help spread the word, answer questions, and build excitement!

As part of your messaging, include details such as the presence of food or other amenities, and make sure to note how many spots are open for it. For example, saying, "Space is limited to twenty participants" encourages teachers to register as quickly as possible, and teachers love food, especially free food!

Plan Ahead

The drawback to breaking away from the traditional locations for professional development is that you sometimes must get creative about getting and using the resources and equipment that you need. Make sure you know if the venue you chose has adequate access to the internet. If it lacks necessary supplies, be sure to gather them in advance and have a plan for bringing them with you and how you can make use of them at the venue.

Just as important, make sure you talk to the venue's manager or proprietor about what you need or plan to bring in. For example, a restaurant owner might not be happy with you hanging things on the wall without advance notice. If you're planning to have food, but the establishment doesn't normally allow food, respect that and work with what you can do.

Remind Everyone of the Intent

As your professional development session begins, be up front about what you hope to accomplish: high-quality professional development in a setting that is local, stimulating, and mutually beneficial to the teachers and the community. Other goals could include the following.

- Gaining a deeper understanding of the community that your students live in

- Having participants return to the location at a later time to help the local economy thrive

- Improving the image of the teaching profession by having community members see how hard teachers work and how committed they are to their community

- Stretching teachers out of their comfort zone to gain new knowledge that we can take back to improve our instruction and help our students learn

Before you begin, invite the owner or manager to say a few words about the location and the products or services that it offers. He or she will most likely enjoy the opportunity to meet some of the teachers. At times, members of the community might come and interact with the teachers as well (hopefully not in a way that disrupts the session). This is a fantastic opportunity to engage with them and spark interest in our schools!

Follow Up and Build Community

When the session is over, there is more you can do to help ensure it is a success and to set the stage for future successes with your community-based professional development efforts. For example, in addition to the obvious thank-you note to the establishment that hosts the event, consider sending it a photo of the teachers in action. I've found that when you email someone a photo as thanks, that person is very grateful. When you send him or her a framed photo, he or she is ecstatic, and will often hang it on the establishment's wall. Imagine every patron who walks into a local business seeing a photo of teachers in action. That's a win-win for the teaching profession and the business.

Also, encourage teachers to return to the establishment on their own and to tell the staff there that they attended the event and are returning because of it. As your colleagues realize the benefits of quality community-based professional development event, you can make use of their enthusiasm by having them act as location scouts who will let you know if they happen to be somewhere that might make a good location for another event.

You can further build on the event by creating a learning team that encourages the teachers who participated to stay in touch with each other. Start an email list, a Facebook page, or a team Slack, which can greatly extend the life of each experience and even make it self-sustaining, as it's no longer one person leading the way. Participants can utilize these to share ideas, ask questions, and think beyond the one event. And remember, everybody loves photos! Posting them on the school or district website shows that you had fun and learned a lot and gets people excited to come to the next event.

Summary

As you begin to implement community-based professional development, remember to get creative and dream big. For example, our history teachers held an event in our city's history museum, teachers interested in learning about using Pinterest for education (www.pinterest.com/teachers) met in the private room of a newly opened café, and a group of our physical education teachers treated each other to a day of learning at the stadium where our professional baseball team (the San Diego Padres) plays.

Whatever you decide, just imagine the energy of an Apple Store as you envision your next professional development. The time has come to break free from the traditional, often stifling, ways and places that are used to provide professional development for teachers and open up to new places and ways of relating.

Our communities, schools, staff, and students ultimately benefit from community-based professional development.

Reflection Questions

Now that you have completed the chapter, consider and reflect on the following questions.

1. What have been your experiences with attending professional development? What do you find determines whether a professional development session is effective or ineffective?

2. What are some locations in the community surrounding your school that might make a nice place to conduct community-based professional development? What specific topic or topics would be a good fit for this location, and who would be a great presenter?

3. What are some strategies you can use to get the word out about your community-based professional development event and generate excitement for it from your colleagues?

4. In addition to implementing community-based professional development, what are some other ways that you could help make your next professional development experience more engaging?

TEACHING TEACHERS
Step Up and Share Your Ideas
With Fellow Educators

Professional development isn't the only way for teachers to engage in lifelong learning with regard to their craft. For example, there are thousands of books, experts, and philosophies out there that guide us in how to best teach our students. These are great resources you can tap, but I truly believe that we teachers learn, implement, and assess the strategies that work best by turning to *each other*, especially when we're in the same room together. It is in collaboration with your colleagues that you take the ideas you find in the work and research of published experts and adapt them for your school culture and community context. It is then, in sharing these ideas and lessons with not only your closest colleagues but the wider teaching community, that you deepen your development as a teacher in real and transformative ways.

As classroom teachers, we know that what works with one student might not work with another, and what works on Monday might bomb on Friday. But as we teach, day after day, and year after year, we've all found that within our successes are *strategies, tips, and advice that work*.

In this chapter, I examine the importance of taking these things that will help your colleagues develop their craft and turning them into official presentations that are sure to produce results. I then offer two highly effective categories of strategies for success that will help you develop an effective presentation by preparing *before* the conference or meeting and then for presenting *at* the event.

The Importance of Sharing Your Knowledge

Just as it's our responsibility as teachers to do everything we can to ensure that our students learn, it's also our responsibility as professionals to share our ideas with other teachers, so that *their* students can benefit as well.

I don't just mean the casual conversations that happen in staff lounges, hallways, and school parking lots, as great as those are. I'm talking about stepping up to share what you know in more formal settings—places such as scheduled staff meetings, local and national conferences, and professional development events. And keep in mind—an effective video of a teacher sharing a strategy has the potential to reach thousands, if not millions, of people!

Ask yourself the following questions: "Don't I have some experience or wisdom I can share more formally with fellow teachers? Have I thought about applying to present at a meeting or conference but haven't taken the leap yet?"

Besides being a service to fellow teachers, I've found that becoming a teacher of teachers can be a wonderful way to reinvigorate yourself professionally—remembering why you chose to teach and how far you've come in doing it. Furthermore, if you find yourself thriving at it, you can advance to more and larger venues. Teaching teachers can even become that important second income stream many of us rely on to pay our bills, while at the same time, it elevates our profession, increases teachers' knowledge, and has a profound effect on our students!

Strategies for Success—How to Get the Gig

To encourage you to just do it and share with other teachers in a more official way the wisdom you've gained in your classroom, I want to share some step-by-step strategies to make it happen. Let's start by talking about how you get yourself on the agenda *before* the event—how to come up with what you can share and how to find someone who wants you to share it. The following are four strategies to get the gig.

Pick Your Topic

Before you do anything, decide what you would like to present on. Sometimes, this is an easy decision. Maybe your principal notices you doing something well and asks you to present. Maybe you have a particular area of interest that you want to explore and evangelize about to others. Regardless, if you're having trouble deciding, ask yourself the following questions.

- "What am I most passionate about in education?"
- "What do I do well in my own classroom, on campus, or within my education community?"
- "What have other teachers consistently asked me to share with them over the years?"

As motivational speaker Les Brown says, "You don't have to be great to get started, but you have to get started to be great" (Goodreads, n.d.a). By answering these three questions, you can get started on the path of sharing with others. Keep in mind that, over time, your topic (or topics) will evolve and grow, and as it does, so will your level of expertise.

Write Your Blurb

Once you've identified your topic, begin to develop your presentation or workshop concept by selecting a clear and engaging title and writing a two-hundred-word description of what you'll cover. When it comes time to make your pitch, some conferences will require a description with fewer words, but once you lay this foundation, you can modify your description as necessary. Picking a catchy title always helps bring attention and audience members to your workshop or gets colleagues a bit more excited.

When possible, tie in your presentation with the conference theme, or the job titles of those who will be in attendance. Also, make sure that you are very clear in the description about what you will be covering and what new knowledge, strategies, or skills your attendees will walk away with. If possible, find an agenda from the previous year's conference, and study the types of titles and descriptions its presenters included. This will give you a very good idea on how to write and structure your title and description.

Here are a few examples of titles that worked very well for me.

- *Creating a Culture of Compassion*
- *How to Connect Math and Literacy: Get Students Reading, Writing and Speaking in Math Class*
- *Owning It: Proven Strategies to Ace and Embrace Teaching* (Sound familiar?)

Make Your Pitch

Find a meeting or conference at which you would like to present. Types of presentations can include lectures; interactive workshops; panel discussions; poster sessions;

and quick, TED-style talks. Finding local, regional, and national conferences is easy to do—just ask some of your colleagues what their favorite conferences are to attend and then look up their respective websites. A simple internet search will also reveal pretty much every type of conference you can imagine.

I highly recommend starting with a local conference in your area. Submitting a proposal can vary from simply contacting the event organizer and asking to present to filling out an official proposal, usually called a request for proposal (RFP) or an abstract. Submission instructions, as well as criteria, are usually on the event website. Each conference has a committee that selects presenters and usually has a window of time within which you can submit your proposal.

Be Easy

This one is simple. If the committee or person you submitted to accepts your proposal, be sure to submit all the information the conference organizers request from you in a timely, organized, and friendly manner. Remember, conference organizers are extremely busy and overwhelmed. Showing them you are easy to work with will solidify your reputation as a professional.

There is, of course, the possibility that your proposal will not be accepted. Don't obsess over rejection! Instead, use that growth mindset and see if you can improve on it for next time. I once emailed the selection committee and asked how I could strengthen my proposal for next time. (Notice I didn't ask, "Why was I rejected?") I received a nice email response, letting me know that my proposal was too similar in nature to several others. I rethought, rewrote, and resubmitted that following year and got accepted.

Strategies for Success—What to Do Once You've Got the Gig

Once you've successfully used the strategies in this chapter to get the gig—and I'm sure you'll be scheduled to speak to fellow teachers in no time—it's time to focus on making a true impact at the event. Here are five strategies for succeeding with your presentation.

Be Prepared and Flexible

When a conference or committee accepts your proposal, it will almost surely provide you with a point of contact. Take advantage of this! Talk to him or her to determine and communicate what equipment you will need to deliver a smashing presentation. Sometimes hosts provide useful tools like projectors, screens, and chart paper. Sometimes they don't. Know in advance what you will (and will not) have access to. Even when you think there are resources you are going to have, be prepared for them to work or not work. Technology is a fickle thing, and you should always have a backup plan in case a tool you planned to use does not function or is unexpectedly unavailable.

Also, think in advance about what you will wear. Conference rooms often run cold to accommodate the many people sitting together. At the same time, many presenters run warm, as the energy required to present makes many people (including me) very hot! Select an outfit that allows you to move comfortably but that also matches the vibe and message you are trying to send. Remember, you have to look the part (see page 158).

Go Early

On the day of your presentation, try to get to the conference or meeting with plenty of time to spare. Even after gathering as much information about the venue as you can, there is no substitute for taking it all in firsthand. Whenever possible, I like to take a peek at the room I'll be presenting in so that I can begin to get comfortable with the surroundings. If there is another presenter in the room at the time, I try to listen to him or her for a bit, noticing things like lighting, acoustics, and seating arrangements. In addition, venues often experience technical difficulties of one sort or another (such as a heating or cooling system not working), and you want to know about them as soon as possible so you can adjust. If you can, check out your audio-visual equipment, and if you are using slides or videos, give them a test run. Give the microphone a test run as well to make sure the volume levels are appropriate. This will also help cut down on nervousness.

Learn by Doing

People don't start off as effective presenters, so it's important to have a growth mindset about your presentation abilities. Pay attention during your presentation. What is going well? What might you improve? Did the audience laugh at a joke? Did they seem bored or skeptical during a particular part?

The first conference presentation I ever gave, *Making Math Cool,* is one that I still give today (Kajitani, 2007). However, each time I present it, I notice something I can tweak or reorganize to be more effective. This is a never-ending process, but I guarantee you that my presentation is a lot better now than when I first gave it!

Tell Stories and Connect the Dots

Whenever possible, make connections to things you heard other conference speakers say or the school goals. Tell stories that highlight the concepts you are speaking about. These can include stories about your students, about your successes and failures as a teacher, or about the challenges we face every single day as teachers. Tell the stories that make us laugh, make us cry, or even make us mad. Stories allow us to make the connections between the content we're presenting and the students we're affecting.

Have Fun

Wherever it is that you're presenting, soak it in and enjoy it. Remember, it's perfectly normal (and often expected) to get nervous. I always suggest that any time you find yourself wanting to say, "I'm so nervous," instead exclaim, "I'm so excited!" Just that small word change can shift your energy.

In addition, if you're presenting at your school, ask your colleagues for their thoughts and opinions, and when possible, involve them in activities. At conferences, sit in on other presentations, introduce yourself to the people you're sitting with, and eat lunch with people you've never met before. Take what you learn from others and share it with colleagues at your school.

Summary

As teachers, we stand in front of our students each day and teach the compelling ideas and concepts that they need to learn. As educators, the time has come for more of us to step up and present to our colleagues throughout the profession what we know works to engage students in learning and achieving.

Our students, our schools, and our profession stand to benefit!

Reflection Questions

Now that you have completed the chapter, consider and reflect on the following questions.

1. What ideas, tools, or strategies do you use that others have said you should share? Have you shared them in a formal setting? If so, where? If not, where might be a good place to start?

2. Are there local, regional, or national conferences that you might like to present at? Consider looking at their event websites and finding out when their next conferences are and how to apply to be a presenter.

3. What are your greatest fears that might hold you back from sharing your ideas with your colleagues? What might be a solution to overcome these fears?

4. What contacts have you made in working with event organizers or when working with other teachers? How might you tap their knowledge and experience to improve your presenting skills?

THE 5-5-5 OF TEACHER BLOGS

Use Blogs to Learn, Share, and Influence Others

Living in an information age, it is critical that teachers find ways to stay constantly informed. At the copier one morning, a colleague asked me what I thought of recent federal education legislation proposals. "Uh . . ." I stumbled, as I had not yet read up on the details. "I don't know. Let me get back to you on that." I immediately ran to my laptop to get informed.

Although I realized later that I should have immediately asked my colleague for his thoughts, a quick check of the proposed legislation gave me all the facts. But what I really needed were the well-formed thoughts, opinions, and dwellings of my fellow teachers. I turned immediately to some teacher-written blogs I highly respect. Within a few clicks, I found myself informed, opinionated, and ready to speak on the issue.

Blogs are a popular way to share information, advertise businesses, and analyze topics that are important to us as teachers. The catch with bloggers is that although they are not necessarily people with a journalistic background, very often the best bloggers (and you do have to be selective) *are* experts in the subject matter they blog about. They know the history, they know the research, and they often know how to interpret complicated data and explain them for the rest of us. No, they're not always balanced, and they aren't beholden to the kinds of ethics rules a professional journalist strives for; however, they are an excellent way to obtain information and opinions, often written in an uncensored, raw, and real fashion that conveys understanding of the topic area better than many mainstream journalists ever will.

In this chapter, I offer three strategies for success related to understanding blogging as a platform, finding some great blogs to learn from, and getting started with your own blog. Each of these strategies has five core aspects, which I call the 5-5-5 of teacher blogs.

Strategies for Success

The following strategies focus on establishing five reasons blogs are an important resource for educators, five existing blogs that are worth following, and five steps to building your own blog.

Five Reasons Blogs Are Important

Whether we consult teacher- or education-focused blogs to learn new skills or to know that we're not alone in our struggles, tapping into the wisdom of our colleagues is a great way to build connections and expertise. Here are five reasons blogs belong in the world of education.

1. **Inspiration:** As teachers, our job can, at times, be difficult and depressing. Reading the real experiences of others helps us stay motivated, compare experiences, and put into perspective the daily challenges we all face.

2. **Insight:** Sometimes there are issues in education that we just don't know much about. Reading blogs not only helps you wade through an abundance of information but often helps develop your own opinions about an education-related topic. This, in turn, helps you articulate those thoughts to others. I often find myself saying, "Oh, that makes sense," or "I totally agree (or disagree) with that person," after reading some of the blogs I mention in the next strategy. Note that the key to identifying a good blogger isn't finding a voice you always agree with, but someone who presents such a clear picture of the topic that you can form your own informed opinion independent of the blogger's take.

3. **Dialogue:** Most blogs feature a comments section that allows you to respond to an author's post. Often, the author will respond back as will other readers. Author participation often depends on the size of the blog's

audience. The larger the audience, the less likely a blogger will devote the time and energy necessary to interact with everyone. A quick check of the comments section will usually indicate how responsive that person is (as well as the quality of his or her audience).

Here is the great thing about interacting with bloggers and other professionals who follow them: they make geographical distance, which once prevented us from interacting with those outside of our school districts, a thing of the past. Blogs open up dialogue among teachers everywhere, shattering former barriers. If you especially like a particular blogger, you can often subscribe to his or her blog, so each time something new is posted, you'll be immediately notified by email. In fact, there are tools (called aggregators) that allow you to follow multiple blogs all in one place. One such tool, Feedly (https://feedly.com), is an excellent platform for subscribing to and following the content at any regularly updated website, including professional news sites and blogs.

4. **Community:** Having a hard time connecting with other science teachers at your school site? Blogs allow you to gain insight from like-minded teachers all over the country. Not sure what to do about that student who is chronically tardy? Chances are, someone's blogged about it. Blogs allow you access to an instant community, regardless of how that community defines itself.

5. **Professional development:** Not sure how to use your interactive whiteboard? Need help teaching your students to add fractions with unlike denominators? Reading blogs is free and easy, and you can often find the information you need to introduce yourself to new teaching concepts without having to drive to, sit through, and then not use the information from that professional development seminar at the district office that your principal just sent you to. (You know it's true!)

Five Blogs You Should Be Reading

Ready to start reading? Here are five blogs (in no particular order) that offer fantastic, deep, and real insight into the world of teaching. They feature content written from some of our country's finest educational bloggers, all of whom are or were classroom teachers.

1. **Nancy Flanagan:** *Teacher in a Strange Land* **(http://blogs.edweek .org/teachers/teacher_in_a_strange_land)**—Nancy Flanagan is the

1993 Michigan Teacher of the Year and a thirty-year veteran K–12 music teacher. She offers sharp-eyed perspectives on the inconsistencies and inspirations and the incomprehensible, immoral, and imaginative in American education. While reading, I often find myself laughing out loud, clenching my jaw, or thinking, "Jeez, she says it so much better than I ever could." Often, I find myself back at work the next day, seeing firsthand exactly what she was talking about.

2. **Bill Ferriter:** *The Tempered Radical* **(http://blog.williamferriter.com)**— Bill Ferriter is a full-time sixth-grade teacher and Solution Tree author. His blog has earned broad recognition for its irreverent takes on topics ranging from the role of media specialists in the public schoolhouse to the damage standardized testing programs do to students. With a commitment to sharing what he knows about 21st century learning and a determination to bridge the gap between policymakers and classroom teachers, Ferriter's work is at once practical and entertaining.

3. **Heather Wolpert-Gawron:** *Tweenteacher* **(http://tweenteacher.com /blog)**—By day, Heather Wolpert-Gawron is a seventh- and eighth-grade language arts, speech, and debate teacher, but at night, she becomes Tweenteacher, blogging the latest news in educational policy and curriculum design and explaining how to more deeply enjoy this crazy and difficult calling of ours. She is always pushing us to continue to develop or reignite our love for teaching, with all its obstacles and insults. Her ultimate focus, and what keeps me coming back, is that she is utterly devoted to developing our students' love of learning. She's especially effective at helping new educators, veterans, and second-career teachers navigate through this difficult yet rewarding career by helping us all challenge past practices in our schools that do not work while highlighting those that do.

4. **National Network of State Teachers of the Year:** *Teacher Leader Voices* **(www.nnstoy.org/blogs/member-blog)**—At this blog, past and present state teachers of the year from around the country weigh in on the most pressing issues in K–12 education, from policy to practice to advocacy. They share their most promising practices, deepest insights, and opinions on what is happening in the classroom and beyond. Teacher Leader Voices is also an excellent example that a blog does not need to have just one author—it regularly rotates posts each week among several teachers. This is

something to consider if you want to try blogging yourself and know other colleagues who would like to contribute!

5. **Rick Hess:** *Straight Up* **(http://blogs.edweek.org/edweek/rick_hess_ straight_up)**—With his blog hosted at Education Week, Rick Hess is the director of education policy studies at the Washington D.C.–based American Enterprise Institute think tank. There, he offers straight talk on matters of policy, politics, research, and reform. Hess, a former high school teacher, influential author, and occasional college professor, brings an acerbic, national perspective to issues like governance, teacher evaluation, the use of evidence, and the Common Core. He's never warm and fuzzy, and some practitioners can sometimes find him infuriating, but he writes with a measured, hardheaded tone that makes his voice distinctive and influential in national policy debates. Remember, you don't have to agree with a blogger's perspective to derive real value from his or her work!

These blogs represent a miniscule slice of the amount of blogging content teachers produce every day, so if you know of a not-to-be-missed teacher blog, be sure to contact me so I can share it with my friends and colleagues!

Five Steps to Start Your Own Blog

As you read and absorb the work of other teacher bloggers, don't be surprised to find that it starts stirring a desire to find and express your own voice and ideas. When that urge to say something about the world of teaching and education spurs your interest to start your own blog, here are five steps to kick off and develop your process, establishing your own platform for dialogue and change.

1. **Pick a topic area and a name:** With all the blogging content available online, it's important to think hard about your message and the way you want to deliver it. Consider the highly successful blogs you turn to, and how each of them likely has its own unique angle or approach. Although you should develop a blog that is uniquely you, and that you're comfortable sharing, think also about your knowledge, experience, and personal style and how you might best convey them in a way that's different from everyone else. When you find this approach, you're ready to give yourself a name (a brand) that is uniquely yours. The more intriguing, the better, but pick something that can act as a unifying theme for all your blog entries.

2. **Pick a portal:** All blogs exist on what we call a portal or host. Two of the most popular and easiest to get started with are WordPress (https://wordpress.com) and Blogger (www.blogspot.com), but there are other good options as well—just ask (or google) around! Getting your blog up and running can range from being free and simple to being rather expensive and complex. Of course, I recommend keeping it as simple as possible at the beginning, and learning, growing, and improving along the way.

3. **Build your readership base:** Much as your content might deserve it, readers are not going to immediately flock to your blog. It takes time to build an audience, so you have to be prepared for good work to not reach a lot of people. One of the best ways to start is tell your friends, family, and colleagues. Ask for feedback and, if they like what they see, ask them to help share and promote your blogs to their professional network. Also, take advantage of every opportunity you have to share your blog with your social media contacts (especially on Twitter) and other professionals you come across, and encourage them to recommend your blog to others!

4. **Use your time strategically:** The thought of writing a new post every week (or however often you choose) might be intimidating. Sure, there will be times when something happens in the news, and you are moved to write a post and quickly share your thoughts. However, the majority of your blog posts might not necessarily be time sensitive, so consider writing several posts in one sitting and then releasing them once a week. As your readership grows, one thing is certain: they'll want more! In a media-driven world, the internet seems to have an insatiable appetite for new content. Find an approach to producing content that keeps you motivated and excited rather than always trying to keep up.

5. **Go beyond words:** The written word is great, but we live in a multimedia-driven era, so consider including pictures, music, videos, coupons, and other items of interest on your blog. Going beyond just writing will help keep your blog fresh and entertaining, and it will give your readers a reason to come back for more!

Summary

There are a lot of people who have something to say about teachers and the state of education these days. But are they teachers? Are they the ones doing the day-to-day work of educating our students? Not enough of them. With legislators making so many decisions that affect the work we do in our classrooms, it is more important than ever for teachers to make their voices heard and help other teacher voices be heard. Whether you're using blogs to gather information, speak your mind, or champion a cause, this form of communication offers a chance to make a measurable contribution to your profession. Happy blogging!

Reflection Questions

Now that you have completed the chapter, consider and reflect on the following questions.

1. Do *you* read any education blogs? If so, which ones? Be sure to share your favorites with your colleagues and with me.

2. What do you see as both the benefits and drawbacks of reading blogs? How do you determine if the information is based on fact or opinion?

3. If you were to start your own blog, what topics do you envision writing about? Who would be your main audience?

4. What are some ways that you can spread the word about your blog or other blogs that you enjoy reading?

EPILOGUE

People often ask me why I teach. I tell them, "Because I want to live forever."

Machines fall apart. Money runs out. Beauty fades. Our ideas are the only true possessions we can pass down from one generation to next. As teachers, we give our students the ideas, skills, and inspiration that they will need to live their lives, pursue their dreams, and create true change in the world. Everything that humans have ever accomplished began with an idea.

I hope that *Owning It* has given you some fresh ideas or a new perspective, or encouraged you to take a risk and try something new in the name of passing your own ideas along to the students you teach. I hope the stories I've told have confirmed that, while the work we do each day is difficult, it is also worth it. I hope the strategies for success I've offered give you the inspiration and the practical tools necessary to be highly effective in the work that you do. Finally, I hope that the reflection questions in each chapter have allowed you a moment to pause, take a deep breath, and look honestly on this work so that you can continue to help improve the lives of your students and help them improve the lives of others.

Over the years, I've had the opportunity to learn from some truly phenomenal teachers. Some were my own teachers, as I navigated the often-tricky landscape of my own education. Some were my colleagues (and continue to be), as we bump up against challenges on a daily basis and work together to find solutions that move our work forward. But above all, I've learned the most from my students. They are the true teachers. They are the ones who, on a daily basis, keep us humble, make us frustrated, demand that we pay attention, and bring us a deep sense of pride to be standing in front of and among them each and every day. Every idea we share with them is an opportunity to create the world *as it can be*.

When we teach, we live forever.

Thanks for reading.

REFERENCES AND RESOURCES

Abrams, J. (2009). *Having hard conversations*. Thousand Oaks, CA: Corwin Press.

Alderman, L. (2016, November 9). Breathe. Exhale. Repeat: The benefits of controlled breathing. *The New York Times*. Accessed at www.nytimes.com/2016/11/09/well /mind/breathe-exhale-repeat-the-benefits-of-controlled-breathing.html on April 12, 2018.

Allday, R. A., & Pakurar, K. (2007). Effects of teacher greetings on student on-task behavior. *Journal of Applied Behavior Analysis, 40*(2), 317–320.

Amos, J. (2014). Teacher attrition costs united states up to $2.2 billion annually, says new alliance report. *Straight As, 14*(14). Accessed at https://all4ed.org/articles /on-the-path-to-equity-teacher-attrition-costs-united-states-up-to-2-2-billion -annually-says-new-alliance-report on November 30, 2017.

Auguste, B. G., Hancock, B., & Laboissiere, M. (2009). *The economic cost of the US education gap*. Accessed at www.mckinsey.com/industries/social-sector /our-insights/the-economic-cost-of-the-us-education-gap on April 12, 2018.

Barnes, G., Crowe, E., & Schaefer, B. (2007). *The cost of teacher turnover in five school districts: A pilot study*. Arlington, VA: National Commission on Teaching and America's Future. Accessed at https://nctaf.org/wp-content/uploads/2012/01 /NCTAF-Cost-of-Teacher-Turnover-2007-full-report.pdf on November 30, 2017.

Billings, S. B., & Schnepel, K. (2017). *Life after lead: Effects of early interventions for children exposed to lead*. Accessed at https://papers.ssrn.com/sol3 /papers.cfm?abstract_id=2998982 on April 9, 2018.

Branson, R. (2015). *Top 6 tips to screw business meetings as usual*. Accessed at www .linkedin.com/pulse/20130215121303-204068115-top-5-tips-to-screw-business -meetings-as-usual on December 18, 2017.

Brown, J., Isaacs, D., Vogt, E., & Margulies, N. (2002). Strategic questioning: Engaging people's best thinking. *The Systems Thinker, 13*(9), 5.

Burmeister, M. (2008). *From boomers to bloggers: Success strategies across generations.* Fairfax, VA: Synergy Press.

California Department of Education. (n.d.). *California High School Exit Examination.* Accessed at www.cde.ca.gov/ta/tg/hs on April 12, 2018.

California Department of Education (2008). *School report—API growth and targets met.* Accessed at https://api.cde.ca.gov/AcntRpt2007/2007GrowthSch .aspx?allcds=37680986038210 on June 26, 2018.

Christ, T., & Wang, X. C. (2010). Bridging the vocabulary gap: What the research tells us about vocabulary instruction in early childhood. *Young Children, 65*(4), 84–91.

Cross, W. E., Jr. (1991). *Shades of black: Diversity in African-American identity.* Philadelphia: Temple University Press.

Data. (n.d.). In *Merriam-Webster's online dictionary.* Accessed at www.merriam -webster.com/dictionary/data on March 19, 2018.

Delpit, L. (2012). *"Multiplication is for white people": Raising expectations for other people's children.* New York: New Press.

Depka, E. (2015). *Bringing homework into focus: Tools and tips to enhance practices, design, and feedback.* Bloomington, IN: Solution Tree Press.

Dilworth, M. E. (Ed.). (2018). *Millennial teachers of color.* Cambridge, MA: Harvard Education Press.

Divergent thinking. (n.d.) In *Collins English dictionary online.* Accessed at www .collinsdictionary.com/dictionary/english/divergent-thinking on December 18, 2017.

Dunckley, V. L. (2014, September 15). Why CFL's aren't such a bright idea [Blog post]. Accessed at www.psychologytoday.com/us/blog/mental-wealth/201409 /why-cfls-arent-such-bright-idea on April 12, 2018.

Dweck, C. S. (2006). *Mindset: The new psychology of success.* New York: Random House.

Educational Research Newsletter & Webinars. (n.d.). *The four characteristics of 'authentic learning.'* Accessed at www.ernweb.com/educational-research-articles/the-four-characteristics-of-authentic-learning/ on November 29, 2017.

Fisher, D., & Frey, N. (2014). *Checking for understanding: Formative assessment techniques for your classroom* (2nd ed.). Alexandria, VA: Association for Supervision and Curriculum Development.

Fisher, D., Frey, N., & Rothenberg, C. (2008). *Content-area conversations: How to plan discussion-based lessons for diverse language learners.* Alexandria, VA: Association for Supervision and Curriculum Development.

Gladwell, M. (2002). *The tipping point: How little things can make a big difference.* New York: Back Bay Books.

Goodreads. (n.d.a). *Les Brown > quotes > quotable quote.* Accessed at www.goodreads.com/quotes/188863-you-don-t-have-to-be-great-to-get-started-but on June 29, 2018.

Goodreads. (n.d.b). *Rita Mae Brown > quotes > quotable quote.* Accessed at www.goodreads.com/quotes/27183-if-it-weren-t-for-the-last-minute-nothing-would-get on June 28, 2018.

Goodreads. (n.d.c). *Theodore Roosevelt > quotes > quotable quote.* Accessed at www.goodreads.com/quotes/118880-no-one-cares-how-much-you-know-until-they-know on April 12, 2018.

Guru: Joseph Juran. (2009, June 19). *The Economist.* Accessed at www.economist.com/node/13881008 on November 29, 2017.

Harney, K. R. (2013, October 4). School quality is tied to home prices in new study. But other factors may affect values. *The Washington Post.* Accessed at www.washingtonpost.com/realestate/school-quality-is-tied-home-prices-in-new-study-but-other-factors-may-affect-values/2013/10/02/f7b12e24-2aa4-11e3-8ade-a1f23cda135e_story.html on April 10, 2018.

Hart, B., & Risley, T. R. (2003). The early catastrophe: The 30 million word gap by age 3. *American Educator, 27*(1), 4–9.

Hierck, T. (2017). *Seven keys to a positive learning environment in your classroom.* Bloomington, IN: Solution Tree Press.

Jackson, S. M. (2012). *Parent, student, and teacher perceptions of student-led conferences and strategies to host effective student-led conferences* (Doctoral dissertation). Accessed at https://search.proquest.com/docview/1426846273 on December 14, 2017.

Kajitani, A. (2004). *Ethnic identity development in middle school.* (Unpublished master's thesis). San Diego State University, California.

Kajitani, A. (2006). It's test tiiiiime!!! On *The Rappin' Mathematician: Volume 1* [CD]. Delair, NJ: Oasis CD Manufacturing.

Kajitani, A. (2007). *Making math cool.* Presentation, San Diego, CA.

Kelling, G. L., & Coles, C. M. (1996). *Fixing broken windows: Restoring order and reducing crime in our communities.* New York: Touchstone.

Kurzweil, R. (2001, March 7). *The law of accelerating returns* [Blog post]. Accessed at http://www.kurzweilai.net/the-law-of-accelerating-returns on May 31, 2018.

La Duke, P. (2016, October 18). Managing conflict is essential to success. *Entrepreneur.* Accessed at www.entrepreneur.com/article/283587 on June 28, 2018.

Lahey, J. (2016, May 4). *To help students learn, engage the motions* [Blog post]. Accessed at http://well.blogs.nytimes.com/2016/05/04/to-help-students-learn -engage-the-emotions on July 3, 2018

Lamperes, B. (1994). Empowering at-risk students to succeed. *Educational Leadership, 52*(3), 67–70.

Lewis, B. (2017). *How to create teachable moments in the classroom.* Accessed at www .thoughtco.com/what-is-a-teachable-moment-2081657 on April 10, 2018.

Lewis, M. (2003). *Moneyball: The art of winning an unfair game.* New York: Norton.

Lyman, F. T. (1981). The responsive classroom discussion: The inclusion of all students. In A. S. Anderson (Ed.), *Mainstreaming digest: A collection of faculty and student papers* (pp. 109–113). College Park, MD: University of Maryland Press.

Mackay, H. (2005). *Swim with the sharks without being eaten alive: Outsell, outmanage, outmotivate, & outnegotiate your competition* (HarperBusiness Essentials ed.). New York: Morrow.

Matson, E. (1996, April 30). The seven sins of deadly meetings. *Fast Company.* Accessed at www.fastcompany.com/26726/seven-sins-deadly-meetings on December 18, 2017.

Mehta, A. (n.d.). *Breaking someone's sugar habit—Gandhi's story* [Blog post]. Accessed at www.avani-mehta.com/2008/08/14/breaking-someones-sugar-habit -gandhis-story on July 3, 2018.

Mizell, H. (2010). *Why professional development matters.* Oxford, OH: Learning Forward. Accessed at https://learningforward.org/docs/default-source/pdf/why _pd_matters_web.pdf on June 26, 2018.

National Center for Educational Statistics. (2015). *Public school teacher attrition and mobility in the first five years: Results from the first through fifth waves of the 2007–08 beginning teacher longitudinal study—First look.* Washington, DC: U.S. Department of Education. Accessed at https://nces.ed.gov/pubs2015/2015337. pdf on December 14, 2017.

National Education Association. (n.d.). *Research spotlight on recruiting and retaining highly qualified teachers.* Accessed at www.nea.org/tools/17054.htm on November 30, 2017.

National Education Association. (2008). *English language learners face unique challenges.* Accessed at www.nea.org/assets/docs/HE/ELL_Policy_Brief_Fall_08 _(2).pdf on December 13, 2017.

Nation's Report Card. (2015). *2015 mathematics & reading assessments.* Accessed at www.nationsreportcard.gov/reading_math_2015/#mathematics/acl?grade=8 on November 30, 2017.

Novak, S., & Slattery, C. (2017). *Deep discourse: A framework for cultivating student-led discussions.* Bloomington, IN: Solution Tree Press.

Ormrod, J. E. (2010). *Characteristics of students at risk and why students drop out.* Accessed at www.education.com/reference/article/characteristics-students -risk on June 26, 2018.

Partnership for 21st Century Learning. (2015). *The 4Cs research series.* Accessed at www.p21.org/our-work/4cs-research-series on April 27, 2018.

Pollock, M. (2004). *Colormute: Race talk dilemmas in an American school.* Princeton, NJ: Princeton University Press.

Rea, D. W. (2015). Interview with Pedro Noguera: How to help students and schools in poverty. *National Youth-At-Risk Journal, 1*(1), 11–21.

Reyes, L. (2015, July 2). *Developing vocabulary for Latino students* [Blog post]. Accessed at www.solutiontree.com/blog/developing-vocabulary-for-latino-students on November 29, 2017.

Salzman, M. (2017, February 10). 5 generations in the workplace (and why we need them all). *Entrepreneur.* Accessed at www.entrepreneur.com/article/288855 on November 30, 2017.

Scott, S. (2017). *Fierce conversations: Achieving success at work and in life one conversation at a time* (New American Library trade paperback edition). New York: New American Library.

Scruggs, A-O. E. (2009, Fall). Colorblindness: The new racism? *Teaching Tolerance,* 36, 45–47. Accessed at www.tolerance.org/magazine/fall-2009/colorblindness-the-new-racism on April 12, 2018.

Sinek, S. (n.d.). *How to listen* [Blog post]. Accessed at http://blog.startwithwhy.com/refocus/2010/06/there-is-a-difference-between-listening-and-waiting-for-your-turn-to---speak-just-because-someone-can-hear-doesnt-mean-t.html on June 25, 2018.

Sitomer, A., & Cirelli, M. (2004). *Hip-hop poetry and the classics.* Beverly Hills, CA: Milk Mug.

Smith, R. (2004). Breaking the cycle of student misbehavior. In R. Smith (Ed.), *Conscious classroom management: Unlocking the secrets of great teaching* (pp. 200–213). Fairfax, CA: Conscious Teaching. Accessed at www.consciousteaching.com/web/wp-content/uploads/CH-13.Breaking-Cycle.CCM_1.pdf on March 12, 2018.

Smith, R., & Dearborn, G. (2016). *Conscious classroom management: Unlocking the secrets of great teaching* (2nd ed.). Fairfax, CA: Conscious Teaching.

Stiggins, R. J., Arter, J. A., Chappuis, J., & Chappuis, S. (2004). *Classroom assessment for student learning: Doing it right—using it well.* Portland, OR: Assessment Training Institute.

Tatum, B. D. (1997). *"Why are all the Black kids sitting together in the cafeteria?" and other conversations about race.* New York: Basic Books.

TED. (2013, May 3). *Every kid needs a champion | Rita Pierson* [Video file]. Accessed at www.youtube.com/watch?v=SFnMTHhKdkw on March 12, 2018.

Thoreau, H. D. (1854). *Walden; or, life in the woods.* Boston: Ticknor and Fields.

Tomlinson, C. A. (2001). *How to differentiate instruction in mixed-ability classrooms* (2nd ed.). Alexandria, VA: Association for Supervision and Curriculum Development.

Troen, V., & Boles, K. C. (2012). *The power of teacher teams: With cases, analyses, and strategies for success.* Thousand Oaks, CA: Corwin Press.

Verhovek, S. H. (1998, January 21). Talk of the town: Burgers v. Oprah. *The New York Times.* Accessed at www.nytimes.com/1998/01/21/us/talk-of-the-town -burgers-v-oprah.html on April 19, 2018.

Watanabe-Crockett, L. (2019). *Future-focused learning: Ten essential shifts of everyday practice.* Bloomington, IN: Solution Tree Press.

WilsonPrep. (2017, September 20). *Working backwards* [Blog post]. Accessed at www.wilsondailyprep.com/working-backwards on May 31, 2018.

Wong, H. K., & Wong, R. T. (2009). *The first days of school: How to be an effective teacher* (4th ed.). Mountain View, CA: Wong.

Wong, H. K., & Wong, R. T. (2014). *The classroom management book.* Mountain View, CA: Wong.

The world's most valuable resource is no longer oil, but data. (2017, May 6). *Economist.* Accessed at www.economist.com/leaders/2017/05/06/the-worlds -most-valuable-resource-is-no-longer-oil-but-data on June 26, 2018.

Zemke, R., Raines, C., & Filipczak, B. (2013). *Generations at work: Managing the clash of boomers, Gen Xers, and Gen Yers, in the workplace* (2nd ed.). New York: American Management Association.

Ziglar, Z. (2002). *Goals: Setting and achieving them on schedule* [Audiobook]. New York: Simon & Schuster Audio.

INDEX

A

Abrams, J., 138
accelerating change, 1
accountability, 3
    for classroom cleaning, 25
    philosophy of teaching and, 9
achievement gap, 4, 49–50
    closing with struggling students, 61–67
    definition of, 61
action plans, 143
aggregators, 187
Alderman, L., 85
Allday, R. A., 16
Alliance for Excellent Education, 64
American Enterprise Institute, 189
analogies, 49–51
Andrews, D. "Coach D," 78–79
anger-management skills, 86–87
Apple stores, 169–170, 175
appreciation, of colleagues, 143
arts, cultural and racial lens on, 74
Artur, J. A., 18
assessments, formative vs. summative, 49–50
at risk students. *See also* challenging students
    being at promise vs., 48
    data in determining, 45–52
attention getting, 17
Auguste, B. G., 4, 49, 61–67
authenticity, 9–13, 18–19
    conflict and, 142
    definition of, 10

B

baby boomers, 131
Barnes, G., 124
Beginning Teacher Support and Assessment
    program, 124
behavior
    confirming without criticizing, 139–140
    environment or health related, 93
    fostering positive, 86
    managing disruptive, 83–90
    offering alternatives to negative, 86–87
    planning for, 87–88
being real, 9–13
    being realistic and, 10, 11
    conflict and, 142
    definition of, 10
    reliability and, 10, 11
    strategies for success in, 10–12
    teaching what is real, 10–11
Blogger, 190
blogs, 100–101, 166, 185–192
    multimedia in, 190
    reasons they are important, 186–187
    steps to starting your own, 189–190
    that you should be reading, 187–189
blurbs, for presentations, 179
Boles, K., 138

Branson, R., 120

broken-windows theory, 21–23

Brown, J., 33

Brown, L., 179

Burmeister, M., 132

Byers, J., 145

C

California Department of Education, 55, 63

California High School Exit Examination, 63

campus tours, 165

challenging students

    closing the achievement gap with, 61–67

    engaging quickly, 16–17

    managing disruptive behavior and, 83–90

    motiving the unmotivated, 77–82

    negotiating with, 91–97

    owning it with, 3–4

    uninvolved parents and, 99–104

Chappuis, J., 18

Chappuis, S., 18

Checking for Understanding (Fisher and Frey), 38–39

checklists, for student-led conferences, 108–109

childcare, 101

clapping

    opening, 17

    two-clap welcome, 95

classroom

    clean floors in, 25

    community visitors to, 166–167

    configuration for student-led conferences, 110–111

    encouraging talking and learning in, 37–44

    first impressions in, 15–20

    order in, 22–27

    presence in, 21–27

Classroom Management Book, The (Wong and Wong), 17

closure, 96

collaboration, 1, 38

    conflicts with colleagues and, 138

    professional development and, 177

colleagues

    conflicts with, 137–144

    generation gaps among, 129–135

    meeting management and, 117–122

colorblind approach to race, 70

Colormute (Pollock), 70

commitment, of ethnicity, 72, 111–112

common ground, 92

communication, 1, 38

    about bias in testing, 56–57

    about your school, 163–168

    blogs, 185–192

    conflict and, 137–144

    creating community allies and, 155–161

    disruptive behavior as, 84

    eye contact in, 24–25, 79

    follow up, in community-based professional development, 174

    generation gaps and, 133

    in job shares, 148–150

    of lesson purpose, 18

    listening in, 42, 142

    making appointments for, 101–102, 140–141

    minimizing negative talk in, 124–125

    in negotiating with students, 91–97

    with parents, 100–101

    practicing skills in, 42

    with quiet students, 65

    rehearsing, 141

    skills, 40, 43, 86–87, 111–112

    student-led conferences and, 107–108

    technology preferences in, 100–101

community

    guest speakers from the, 158

involving in testing, 56
spotlighting your school and, 163–168
teacher blogs and, 185–192
turning foes into allies in, 155–161
community-based professional development,
169–176
follow up after, 174
goals in, 173–174
locations for, 172
planning for, 173
publicizing, 172–173
purpose of, 171
strategies for, 171–174
compassion, 132
conferences
parent-teacher, uninvolved parents and,
100–101
student-led, 105–113
conflict, 137–144
appreciation and follow up on, 143
being specific about, 141–142
confirming behavior without publicly
criticizing, 139–140
job shares and, 147–148
making appointments around, 140–141
perspectives on, 139
planning to deal with, 142–143
rehearsing your approach to, 141
rethinking your approach to, 137–138
conflict-resolution skills, 86–87
connections, with unmotivated students,
77–78
consistency
in job shares, 149, 150
in negotiation, 93–94
contracts, behavior, 94
cooling-off areas, 88
creativity, 38, 119–120
crime, broken-windows theory on, 22
critical thinking, 38
Cross, W. E., Jr., 71–72
Crowe, E., 124

Crum, M., 105
cultural relevance, 63–64, 69–76
culture, compassionate, 132
curriculum, culturally relevant, 63–64,
69–76
customer service, 16

D

Daniels, W. R., 118
data, 45–52
analogies in explaining, 49–51
as conversation starter, 47–48
defining, 46–47
examples of, 47
seeing the students behind, 48
for student-led conferences, 108
using by publicizing, 49
Dearborn, G., 84
debriefing areas, 88
Delpit, L., 74
dialogue, blogs in creating, 186–187
digital natives, 131
discussion, encouraging, 37–44
disruption
managing disruptive behavior and,
83–90
planning for, 87–88
targeting behaviors causing, 21–27
divergent thinking, 119–120
diversity
among colleagues, 4
among students, 1
bias in testing and, 56–57
closing the achievement gap and, 61–67
conflict and, 138
culturally relevant curriculum and,
63–64
ethnic identity and, 69–76
ethnicity formation and, 71–73
generation gaps and, 4–5, 129–135
managing disruptive behavior and, 83

professional development and, 64–65

storytelling about, 157–158

understanding/honoring cultural barriers and, 79

dress, 158–159, 181

Dweck, C. S., 2, 11, 54, 62, 79

E

empowerment of student voices, 166–167

encounter, of ethnicity, 72

engagement

community, 163–167

connecting quickly and, 16

uninvolved parents, 99–104

English language learners (ELLs), 62, 107–108, 110

escalation, preventing, 88

ethnic identity, 69–76

Everyone a Reader, 131

exit tickets, 96

expectations

classroom, 22–23

consistency in, 93–94

posting in the classroom, 149

realistic, 10, 11

external noise, 86

eye contact, 24–25, 40, 79

F

Facebook, 100–101, 174

fear, 163

feedback, 182

Feedly, 187

Ferriter, B., 188

Fierce Conversations (Scott), 142

Filipczak, B., 132

First Days of School, The (Wong and Wong), 94, 148–149

first impressions, 15–20

grabbing their attention and, 17

hypocrisy and, 18–19

providing purpose and, 18

strategies for success in, 16–19

Fisher, D., 38–39, 43

Fisher, P., 83

fixed mindset, 62

Flanagan, N., 188

Frey, N., 38–39, 43

From Boomers to Bloggers: Success Strategies Across Generations (Burmeister), 132

G

Gandhi, M., 19

generation gaps, 4–5, 129–135

acknowledging and celebrating, 132

talking about, 130–132

Generations at Work (Zemke, Raines, and Filipczak), 132

generation X, 131

generation Z, 131

gen next, 131

gen Y, 131

Gladwell, M., 21, 22

goals

generation gaps and, 133–134

for meetings, 118–119

growth mindset, 2, 180

being realistic and, 11

fixed mindset vs., 62

standardized tests and, 54–55

in teachers and students, 79

guest speakers, 120, 158

for community-based professional development, 172

H

Hancock, B., 4, 49, 61–67

Harney, K. R., 53

Hart, B., 62

Having Hard Conversations (Abrams), 138

Hess, R., 189

Hierck, T., 23

Hip-Hop Poetry and the Classics (Sitomer), 74

Hoff, J., 49–50

homework, understanding why it wasn't done, 33–34

humor, 125

hypocrisy, 18–19

I

immersion and emersion, of ethnicity, 72

Immordino-Yang, M. H., 16

incentives, for behavior, 87

insight, 186

inspiration, 186

internalization, of ethnicity, 72

internal noise, 86

interrogator strategy, 40–42

Isaacs, D., 33

J

Jackson, S., 106

job shares, 145–151

    beginning and ending the year together in, 148

    flexibility and limits in, 149–150

    partnership in, 147–148

    planning for, 146–147

    pros and cons of, 146

    written procedures for, 148–149

Juran, J., 4

K

Kajitani, A., 55, 70, 181

Kelling, G., 21–23

kinesthetics, 32

Kurzweil, R., 1

L

Laboissiere, M., 4, 49, 61–67

La Duke, P., 137

Lamperes, B., 77

leadership, 106, 111, 123

learning

    connecting to what students know and, 30

    encouraging talking and, 37–44

    lifelong, 147–148, 177

    by the one talking, 31–32

    stressing testing vs., 30–31

Lewis, B., 29

Lewis, M., 46

lifelong learning, 147–148, 177

lighting, classroom, 86

listening, 42, 142

literacy, 62

Lyman, F., 39

M

Mackay, H., 43

"Making Math Cool" (Kajitani), 181

Margulies, N., 33

marketing, 163–164

MathRaps, 55

McDonald's, 94–95

McKinsey & Company, 61

media, creating allies with, 156–157

meditation, 85

meetings

    cultural importance of, 118

    goals and plans for, 118–119

    guests in, 120

    managing, 117–122

    rewarding creative thought in, 119–120

    routines vs. traditions in, 120–121

Mehta, A., 19

mentors, 133, 135

milestones, celebrating, 125

millennials, 131

Millennial Teachers of Color (Dilworth), 132

Mizell, H., 64

motivation

    encouraging in unmotivated students, 77–82

for positive behavior, 87

through scarcity, 95–96

Multiplication Is for White People (Delpit), 74

N

National Center for Educational Statistics, 64

National Education Association, 62, 123

Diversity Toolkit, 74

National Network of State Teachers of the Year, 188–189

negative talk, minimizing, 124–125

negotiation

from common ground, 92

skills for, 86–87

with struggling students, 91–97

news media, creating allies with, 156–157

Noguera, P., 71

noise, classroom, 86

Novak, S., 38

O

Oakland As, 46

objectives, misaligned, 92

Ormrod, J. E., 45

owning it

being real and, 9–13

with challenging students, 3–4

as a colleague, 4–5

definition of, 2

in your classroom, 3

in your community, 5

P

Pakurar, K., 16

parents

the achievement gap and, 62

communicating with clearly, 164

involving in testing, 56

offering food and childcare to, 101

presenting expectations to, 24

student-led conferences and, 107–108

uninvolved, engaging, 99–104

parent-teacher conferences

job shares and, 150

uninvolved parents and, 100–101

Pareto Principle, 4

Partnership for 21st Century Learning, 38

perceptions

classroom presence and, 22–27

of data, 47, 48

of possibilities in students, 79

perspectives, on conflicts, 139

philosophy of teaching, 9–13

Pierson, R., 77–78

Pincus-Kajitani, M., 145

Pinterest, 174–175

pitches, for presentations, 179

police departments, 64–65

Pollock, M., 70

portals, blog, 190

posture, 85, 91

Power of Teacher Teams, The (Troen and Boles), 138

pre-encounter, ethnicity and, 72

presence, classroom, 21–27

primal screams, 87

procedures, for job shares, 148–149

professional development, 64–65

blogging and, 187

community-based, 169–176

conflicts with colleagues and, 138

generation gaps and, 133

teaching, 177–183

professionalism, 1, 5, 158–159

knowledge sharing and, 177–183

public speaking skills, 43, 109–110, 167, 177–183. *See also* student-led conferences

nerves and, 182

purpose, communicating clearly, 18

R

race and ethnicity, 69–76. *See also* diversity
  how it forms, 71–73
  how to use in the classroom, 73–74
  understanding what it is, 71
Race: The Power of Illusion (TV show), 74
Raines, C., 132
Rappin' Mathematician, The, 55, 80
rapport, 102
Rea, D. W., 71
Reaching At-Promise Students Association
  (RAPSA), 2
real estate values, 53
realistic expectations, 10
reciprocity, 93
rejection, 180
reliability, 10, 11
requests for proposal (RFP), 180
respect, for ethnicity, 73
Reyes, L., 30
Rhoades, J., 145
Risley, T., 62
role models, 80
room configuration, 110–111
Roosevelt, T., 81
Rothenberg, C., 43
routines vs. traditions, 120–121

S

Salzman, M., 130–132
scarcity, motivating through, 95–96
Schaefer, B., 124
schedules, 94, 107
school ratings, 53
Scott, S., 142
Scruggs, A. E., 70
self-control, 85
self-worth, 141–142
Seven Keys to a Positive Learning Environment in Your Classroom (Hierck), 23
Shades of Black (Cross), 71–72

silent generation, 130–131
Sinek, S., 42
Siromer, A., 74
Slack, 174
Slattery, C., 38
Smith, R., 84
social media, 159. *See also* blogs
  Facebook, 100–101, 174
  publicizing professional development
    in, 173
social norms, 79. *See also* diversity
social validation, 94–95
Sonic Pics, 42
Stiggins, R., 18
storytelling, 80, 157–158, 182
Straight Up (Hess), 189
"Strategic Questioning: Engaging People's
  Best Thinking" (Brown, Isaacs, Vogt, and
  Margulies), 33
stress management, 126–127
structured choices, 88
student-led conferences, 105
  checklists for, 108–109
  data gathering for, 108
  date selection for, 107
  rehearsing, 109–110
  room configuration for, 110–111
students
  closing the achievement gap with,
    61–67
  connecting with quickly, 15, 16
  as customers, 15–16
  diversity of, 1
  empowering, 166–167
  greeting at the classroom door, 24–25
  owning it with challenging, 3–4
  quiet, connecting with, 65
  at risk, 45–52
success, celebrating, 125
success stories, 78–79, 80
*Swim With the Sharks Without Being Eaten
  Alive* (Mackay), 43

T

talking. *See also* communication
  encouraging learning and, 37–44
  learning and, 31–32
Tatum, B. D., 74
teachable moments, 29–35
  disruptive behavior and, 87
  encouraging talking and learning in, 37–44
Teacher in a Strange Land (Flanagan), 188
Teacher Leader Voices, 188–189
teachers
  authenticity of, 18–19
  blogs by, 185–192
  celebrating milestones/successes of, 125
  as classroom leaders, 3
  classroom presence of, 21–27
  conflicts between, 137–144
  data perceptions of, 45–52
  decision making by, 125–126
  dress for, 158–159, 181
  first impressions by, 15–20
  generation gaps among, 129–135
  job sharing by, 145–151
  knowledge sharing by and with, 177–183
  learning sabotaged by, 29–35
  meeting management for, 117–122
  negotiating with students, 91–97
  professional development for, 64–65, 169–183
  retaining, 64, 123–128
  self-care for, 126–127
  self-control of, 85
  spotlighting your school and, 163–168
  storytelling by, 80, 157–158
  teaching, 177–183
  value-added evaluation of, 49
  what to say/not say, 29–34
  who leave teaching, 4
teaching
  motivation for, 193
  personal philosophy of, 9–13
  responsibility for learning in, 1
  social media posts about, 159
  turning foes into allies on, 155–161
  what is real, 10–11
Teaching Tolerance, 74
teams, multigenerational, 133
technology
  generation gaps and, 129, 131
  practicing communication skills and, 42
  for presentations, 181
TED Talks, 77–78
tell, ask, connect strategy, 73
temperature, classroom, 86
Tempered Radical, The (Ferriter), 188
tests, 53–58
  bias in, 56–57
  celebration vs. intimidation and, 55
  community involvement with, 56
  improvement vs. perfection as goal of, 54–55
  scores from as data, 46–47
  stressing learning vs., 30–31
"Test Tiiiiime!" (song), 55
think-pair-share strategy, 39–40
Thoreau, H. D., 41
three-question strategy, 40–42
Tipping Point, The (Gladwell), 21
Title I, 163
titles, or presentations, 179
traditionalists, 130–131
traditions vs. routines, 120–121
translators, 110
Troen, V., 138
turning numbers into people, 73–74
Tweenteacher (Wolpert-Gawron), 188
two-clap welcome, 95

V

Verhovek, S. H., 156
visibility, teacher, 21–27
Vogt, E., 33

W

Walden (Thoreau), 41
warm-up activities, 17
Watanabe-Crockett, L., 16
websites, school, 100–101, 165–166
whip arounds, 119
Why Are All the Black Kids Sitting Together in the Cafeteria (Tatum), 74
Wilson, J., 21

WilsonPrep, 54
Winfrey, O., 156
Wolpert-Gawron, H., 188
Wong, H., 17, 94, 148–149
Wong, R., 17, 94, 148–149
WordPress, 190

Z

Zemke, R., 132
Ziglar, Z., 33

The Beginning Teacher's Field Guide
Tina H. Boogren
The joys and pains of starting a teaching career often go undiscussed. This guide explores the personal side of teaching, offering crucial advice and support. The author details six phases every new teacher goes through and outlines classroom strategies and self-care practices.
BKF806

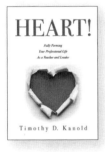

Future-Focused Learning
Lee Watanabe-Crockett
When educators embrace student-centered learning, classrooms transform, learning comes alive, and outcomes improve. With *Future-Focused Learning*, you will discover ten core shifts of practice—along with simple microshifts—that will help take the great work you are already doing and make it exceptional.
BKF807

HEART!
Timothy D. Kanold
Explore the concept of a heartprint—the distinctive impression an educator's heart leaves on students and colleagues during his or her professional career. Use this resource to reflect on your professional journey and discover how to foster productive, heart-centered classrooms and schools.
BKF749

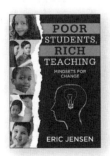

Poor Students, Rich Teaching
Eric Jensen
Discover research-based strategies to ensure all students, regardless of circumstance, are college and career ready. This thorough resource details the necessary but difficult work that teachers must do to establish the foundational changes that positively impact students in poverty.
BKF603

Wait! Your professional development journey doesn't have to end with the last pages of this book.

We realize improving student learning doesn't happen overnight. And your school or district shouldn't be left to puzzle out all the details of this process alone.

No matter where you are on the journey, we're committed to helping you get to the next stage.

Take advantage of everything from **custom workshops** to **keynote presentations** and **interactive web and video conferencing**. We can even help you develop an action plan tailored to fit your specific needs.

Let's get the conversation started.

Call 888.763.9045 today.

SolutionTree.com